"*The Divorce Recovery Workbook* skillfully integrates uncovering feelings, mindfulness, and compassion to allow the reader to navigate the difficult necessity of post-divorce forgiveness. A very thoughtful, useful, and helpful book."

> —**Frederic Luskin, PhD**, director of the Stanford Forgiveness Projects, and author of *Forgive for Good*

"Give this one five stars! Rye and Moore have integrated the most up-to-date psychology research into a down-to-earth, practical workbook filled with user-friendly exercises and a spirit of hope. This will be an invaluable tool for any man or woman struggling with the pain of divorce."

> —**Kenneth I. Pargament, PhD**, professor of psychology at Bowling Green State University, and author of *Spiritually Integrated Psychotherapy*

"In *The Divorce Recovery Workbook*, Rye and Moore provide an excellent applied workbook for you if you've been dealing with the loss of a marriage or long-term relationship. In fact, as I read the manuscript, I could not help but think that the workbook could help deal with many losses, not just divorce. It adapts evidence-based interventions from positive psychology—forgiveness of self and others, gratitude, benefit-finding, happiness, mindfulness, meaning-finding, and self-compassion—into dealing with your loss. It is a wonderful adaptation of respected scholarship so that you can benefit by it."

> —**Everett L. Worthington, Jr., PhD**, professor and director of the counseling psychology program at Virginia Commonwealth University, and author of *Moving Forward*

"Divorce is painful, but it can be navigated with compassion. This wonderful book contains concrete tools that will help you learn how to support yourself through this trying time, so you'll emerge happier, healthier, and whole again."

> —**Kristin Neff, PhD**, associate professor of human development and culture, University of Texas at Austin, and author of *Self-Compassion*

"Divorce is a process that often leaves one emotionally raw, hurt, and angry. It's critical that you take the time to heal from the emotional fallout of divorce—and, all too often, people don't do the work or know what to do. If you want an effective action plan and strategies to move forward to build a better life post-divorce, this book is it! It's a must-read for all my divorce coaching clients."

—**Deborah Moskovitch,** divorce coach and author of *The Smart Divorce*

"Reading the book is a sheer delight. You feel like the authors are sitting and talking with you about the struggles of divorce, and ever so gently and professionally offering a series of well-proven, positive psychology remedies for coping. This is a positive, insightful, and compassionate approach."

—**Loren L. Toussaint, PhD,** associate professor of psychology at
Luther College, and associate director of Sierra Leone Forgiveness Project

"Rye and Moore have developed a powerful and practical resource for those struggling with the pain of divorce. This workbook is personally engaging and easy to read, and it is firmly grounded in empirical research. Rye and Moore manage to strike just the right balance."

—**Julie Exline, PhD,** professor of psychology and director of clinical
training at Case Western Reserve University

The
DIVORCE
RECOVERY
WORKBOOK

how to
heal from anger,
hurt & resentment
& build the life
you want

MARK S. RYE, PhD
CRYSTAL DEA MOORE, PhD

New Harbinger Publications, Inc.

The self-compassion scale in Exercise 3.2 is adapted with permission from the work of Kristin Neff.

Exercise 3.5, "Letting Go of Labels Through Realizing Our Interconnectedness," is adapted from SELF-COMPASSION by Kristin Neff, PhD. Copyright © 2011 by Kristin Neff. Reprinted by permission of HarperCollins Publishers and Hodder and Stoughton Limited.

NEW HARBINGER PUBLICATIONS is a registered trademark of New Harbinger Publications, Inc.

Distributed in Canada by Raincoast Books

Copyright © 2015 by Mark S. Rye and Crystal Dea Moore
New Harbinger Publications, Inc.
5674 Shattuck Avenue
Oakland, CA 94609
www.newharbinger.com

Cover design by Amy Shoup
Acquired by Wendy Millstine
Edited by Brady Kahn

Library of Congress Cataloging-in-Publication Data

Rye, Mark S.
 The divorce recovery workbook : how to heal from anger, hurt, and resentment and build the life you want / Mark S. Rye, Crystal Dea Moore.
    pages cm
 Includes bibliographical references.
 ISBN 978-1-62625-070-3 (paperback) -- ISBN 978-1-62625-071-0 (pdf e-book) -- ISBN 978-1-62625-072-7 (epub)
 1. Divorce--Psychological aspects. 2. Divorced people--Psychology. 3. Adjustment (Psychology) I. Moore, Crystal Dea. II. Title.
 HQ814.R94 2015
 --dc23   2014046562

Printed in the United States of America

24   23   22

10   9   8   7   6   5   4

Crystal would like to dedicate this book to Jeffrey and Gavin and thank them for continuing to teach her the meaning of family and forgiveness.

Mark would like to dedicate this book to his parents, Bob and Francie, who have inspired him to learn positive ways of coping with life's challenges.

Contents

Acknowledgments

Writing this book has given us a wonderful opportunity to practice the positive psychology strategy of gratitude. Many people gave generously of their time and talent to assist us on this project, and we'd like to take a moment to express our appreciation.

We want to begin by thanking our fantastic editorial team at New Harbinger Publications. This book would not have been written without Wendy Millstine, who first approached us about the possibility of writing a book, helped us shape the initial concept, and successfully pitched the book to her colleagues. We're also deeply indebted to Melissa Kirk and her fellow editors who provided us with helpful and encouraging feedback throughout the writing process. They struck a perfect balance between allowing us freedom to find our own style and providing us with invaluable guidance along the way. In addition, we're grateful for the excellent work of our copy editor, Brady Kahn.

We were touched by Teresa Hartnett's generous spirit and her willingness to take time out of her busy schedule to teach us the ins and outs of book publishing. No amount of chocolate chip cookies can adequately compensate Teresa for her assistance, but that won't stop us from sending more.

We appreciate the generous funding that the Fetzer Institute and the John Templeton Foundation provided for our research on forgiveness and postdivorce adjustment.

Several people went above and beyond the call of duty to assist with this project. We can't thank them enough for the assistance they provided. They include Susan Gordon, Rahan Ali,

Neil Cervera, and Peg Tacardon. Thanks to Jeffrey Moore for his cheerleading, baking, editing, and listening throughout the writing process.

We'd like to offer an especially warm thanks to the students at Skidmore College who spent many hours reading drafts and providing suggestions. Their energy, wisdom, enthusiasm, and encouragement helped keep us going. They are a huge part of why we love our jobs as college professors so much. Special thanks go to students in the Skidmore College Positive Psychology Lab: Samantha Fassak, Karen Rothman, Derek Nunner, Max Weigel, Lizzie Dean, Tess Lauricella, Brittany Dingler, Brianna Wellen, Daniel Johnstone, Sophie Byland, Ariel Branden, and Grace Zutrau. We'd also like to give a shout-out to the students from the fall 2013 section of the "Good Life" course for their excellent ideas and for sharing about their experiences conducting community outreach programs on gratitude. Many thanks to Ashley Reynolds for her keen editorial eye and to Randy Castillo for his beautiful illustration in chapter 2.

Finally, and most importantly, we're grateful to the divorced clients, divorced friends, and workshop participants who shared their stories and their struggles with us and who have inspired us with their courage and determination to find healing.

Introduction

There are many books on the market that provide advice on how to find a divorce lawyer, manage financial and custody issues, talk to your kids about divorce, and reenter the dating scene. This isn't one of them. Instead, this book is about developing personal strengths that will enable you to get your moxie back and flourish. Let's face it. Divorce might be one of the most difficult challenges you'll ever encounter. So if you're suffering deeply right now, try not to be too hard on yourself. Who wouldn't be struggling after everything you've been through?

Although developing personal strengths won't make all of your divorce-related problems disappear, it can help you find peace of mind. Learning how to find peace of mind in the midst of life's most tumultuous storms is one of the most beautiful and life-affirming gifts you can give yourself. As your perspective becomes more peaceful, you'll be able to approach the problems that confront you with greater wisdom, clarity, and confidence.

There are many approaches to coping with divorce. The key is to find one that actually works! If you haven't found an effective approach yet and you are willing to do some work on yourself, we invite you to read about how the concepts and techniques from the field of positive psychology can help you. So what is positive psychology?

THE POSITIVE PSYCHOLOGY APPROACH

If you've never heard of positive psychology, we promise that it's not a Pollyannaish approach to solving your problems. It does not involve putting on rose-colored glasses and ignoring emotional pain. Instead, positive psychology is a rapidly growing area of scientific research that examines how personal strengths and virtues can help people thrive.

The positive psychology concepts described in this book are not new ideas. What is relatively new is the commitment by researchers to study personal strengths and virtues from a scientific perspective. Scientists have made exciting recent discoveries about how positive psychology can improve your life. Best of all, positive psychology can help you identify and build upon strengths you already have.

WHO CAN BENEFIT FROM THIS BOOK?

This book is for anyone who is divorced, separated, or breaking up with a long-term romantic partner. It's also for members and leaders of divorce support groups, as well as therapists, divorce educators, and life coaches who are looking for empirically grounded approaches for helping divorced clients.

This book is not intended as a substitute for therapy. Many people find therapy to be an important source of support following divorce, and we encourage you to seek assistance from a therapist if that feels right to you. Moreover, this book can't take the place of a divorce support group. There's nothing quite like spending time with folks who've been through the same painful experiences and who can provide support and encouragement on your journey toward healing. By all means, consider joining a divorce support group if there's a good one nearby.

WHY WE WROTE THIS BOOK

We're both licensed therapists (Mark is a licensed clinical psychologist and Crystal is a licensed clinical social worker) who have worked with divorced clients, and we wanted to share with readers how positive psychology strategies can help facilitate healing after divorce. In our role as college professors, we have published research on applying positive psychology principles to help people cope with divorce, and some of the exercises for this workbook came from a workshop that we developed based on positive psychology techniques. Furthermore, we both have confidence that if you're willing to put in some work, positive psychology strategies can help you make it through this difficult time in your life and move toward healing and greater peace.

WHAT YOU'LL FIND HERE

Discussion of scientific findings. We describe scientific evidence for the effectiveness of positive psychology techniques in a way that's easy to understand. We also include the references in case you want to read the original studies.

Case examples. Throughout the book, we provide case examples to illustrate the types of challenges that divorced individuals commonly face. These examples are loosely based on former clients, workshop participants, and other divorced people we know. Identifying information has been altered and case examples are often composites of the experiences of more than one person. Although not every case will resemble your own circumstances, we trust that something useful can always be gleaned from reading about the experiences of others.

Exercises. This book contains exercises designed to help you reflect deeply about positive psychology concepts and apply them to your life. The exercises will help you remain actively engaged in the healing process.

Suggestions for dealing with obstacles. We can't promise that applying positive psychology strategies to your life will be easy. In fact, sometimes it'll be quite difficult. For this reason, we provide suggestions for handling obstacles that can arise.

Encouragement by the authors. Throughout the book, we'll do our best to encourage you on your journey. You can think of us as your cheerleaders.

HOW TO GET THE MOST OUT OF THIS BOOK

Don't read this book in one sitting. This book is designed to be read over a period of several weeks. Some folks will find it helpful to read one chapter a week. Feel free to pick a pace that is faster or slower, depending on your needs. You'll likely want to linger on some chapters longer than others.

Do your homework. One of our most important pieces of advice is to complete the exercises in each chapter. Reading this book without doing the exercises is like reading about yoga without doing any of the poses. Granted, it's much faster to simply read about the exercises, but the real benefit to you is in the application. So please give the exercises a try. We know that it can be difficult to find time to write. We also understand that some of the exercises may bring up uncomfortable feelings, so it might be tempting to skip them. But try to think of the time you spend completing the exercises as an investment in yourself—and you're worth investing in!

Keep your homework away from your ex, your children, and your nosy neighbor. Many of the exercises in this book are of a deeply personal nature and require a high level of self-disclosure and honesty. Therefore, it's important that you find a safe and secure location to keep your completed homework. You may choose to complete the written exercises in a journal instead of writing your responses directly in the book. Again, wherever you write things down, the most important thing is that you do the exercises!

Share your homework with those you trust. You might find it helpful to share your homework (or portions of your homework) with a trusted friend, a therapist, or members of your divorce support group. They can often provide insights that you don't notice, and sharing what you are working on with others can help you feel less alone on your journey.

IMPORTANT POINTS TO REMEMBER

Take care of yourself. Don't forget—you're in charge of your own healing journey. If any concept or technique makes you feel uncomfortable, it's okay to skip it and move on to something else. You can return to these sections at a later time when you're ready.

Be open to considering a different perspective. One of the keys to improving how you cope with divorce is to be open to considering alternative perspectives. All of us can get caught in the trap of thinking that our version of events is the only reasonable one. We tend to selectively focus on some aspects of what happened while ignoring others. Furthermore, we usually make judgments based on incomplete information. Even the slightest willingness to consider that there are other ways of thinking about your circumstances opens the door to exciting possibilities for changing your life.

Try to let go of things that are out of your control. Naturally, anyone would like to be able to control the events that happen during and after a divorce. Yes, it would be easier if your ex would act the way that you want, the lawyers and the judge would make all of the right decisions, and your kids would stay on their best behavior. In reality, there are aspects of the divorce process that you can't control. This can be anxiety provoking. Trying to control what can't be controlled is of course a losing battle, but that doesn't stop some of us from trying. Instead of worrying about what may be out of your hands, focus on the things you can control that will make your life better. Remember, you can always choose how to think and respond to what's happening, even when the going gets tough.

Keep your sense of humor. In the midst of the most trying times, it's important to keep your sense of humor. Therefore, we've strategically planted a few jokes throughout the book. If you think some of the jokes fall flat, you should've seen the ones that didn't make the final cut!

Ask for help when you need it. We all have moments when we get discouraged and feel overwhelmed. Try to remember that you don't have to travel this journey alone. If you don't have a good support network already, consider reaching out for help and searching for other folks who have traveled down this road.

Try to identify your signature strengths. The founder of positive psychology, Martin Seligman (2002), emphasized the importance of identifying your signature strengths. Signature strengths are ones that you already possess and have used effectively in the past. As you read this book, keep an eye open for the positive psychology topics that play to your strengths, and make a commitment to draw upon them as often as possible as you work toward healing from your divorce.

WHAT'S FIRST?

Before you start applying positive psychology strategies to your life, it's important to take some time to assess your current emotional state. So that's where you'll begin this journey.

CHAPTER 1

"I'm So Upset I Can Hardly Stand It"

Acknowledging and Honoring Your Feelings

Divorce is often referred to as an emotional roller coaster. It's a good analogy. Roller coasters start out on a slow, seemingly harmless climb that can lull riders into a sense of complacency. Suddenly, without much warning, the cars accelerate into terrifying plunges, unexpected turns, and loops that flip you upside down. Similarly, signs of trouble aren't always apparent at the outset of a marriage, and even when they are apparent, people frequently ignore them. When the relationship falls apart, the turmoil can be both sudden and jarring, with emotions changing rapidly with each turn of events. These feelings are especially difficult to deal with if your partner initiated the divorce or hurt you deeply.

This book will focus on positive psychology techniques that can help you cope with difficult emotions related to your divorce. But first we recommend that you reflect on your own emotional state. Using new coping strategies without taking the time to assess your emotional state is like treating a medical condition before understanding the diagnosis. Relapse is more likely because the initial problem was never accurately identified.

> ## Chapter Focus
>
> This chapter will help you reflect on your current emotional state. Although people often experience a wide range of emotions following a divorce, we invite you to focus for now on any feelings of anger, sadness, and anxiety that you have. These are common and understandable reactions to divorce. But when they grow deep roots and play a central role in your postdivorce life outlook, they can cause considerable misery.

ANGER AS A REACTION TO DIVORCE

An online survey conducted by one of our former students, Cara McCabe (2013), found that over 60 percent of divorced individuals believed they had been wronged by their exes. Common transgressions included deceit, infidelity, failure to fulfill obligations, verbal and physical abuse, gossip, and financial misconduct. Given these profoundly hurtful actions, it's not surprising that many people are angry toward their exes. Consider the cases of Diego and Carrie.

The Case of Diego

Diego, who is in his twenties, shared a passion for collecting sports memorabilia with his wife Serena. During their two-year marriage, they amassed an interesting and relatively valuable collection. After Diego moved out and began divorce proceedings, Serena sold the collection on eBay, including an autographed hat that Diego had promised to his Dad, who was terminally ill. Diego was furious at Serena for selling their collection without consulting him. His father died shortly after their divorce. Diego experienced intense anger toward Serena and could not stop thinking about what she had done.

The Case of Carrie

Carrie had been married for twelve years, was deeply in love with her husband Bill, and had what she and many of her friends believed to be a model marriage. Consequently, she was crushed when she learned that her husband had cheated on her with a younger woman and wanted a divorce. Her dream of growing old with him evaporated and was replaced with a profound feeling of loss. After the divorce, she maintained that she wasn't angry but was instead deeply saddened. However, three years later, after one too many bad blind dates, she began to feel rage toward Bill.

Everyone deals with anger differently following divorce. Diego told his friends, family, colleagues, and anyone else who would listen about how angry he was at Serena. Each time he replayed Serena's actions in his mind or retold the story to others, he experienced a surge of anger. In contrast, Carrie told others that she wasn't angry toward her ex. Anger wasn't an emotion that she commonly expressed, nor was it an emotion that she easily recognized. However, her unacknowledged feelings of anger eventually turned into rage that became impossible to ignore.

Regardless of when and why anger is experienced, it's an understandable reaction to harmful actions by your ex. There's no shame in the fact that you're feeling angry, and there's no sense in berating yourself for having these feelings. However, it's important to be aware of your anger so that you can deal with it in an adaptive way.

One way to get in touch with your anger following a divorce is to take an inventory of your grudges. Grudges are like weeds in your garden that start out small and are hard to distinguish from other plants but can eventually take nutrients away from the fruits and veggies that you're trying to grow. If left unattended, they can crowd out adaptive ways of thinking following a divorce. Taking time to reflect on your grudges will help you keep them in check.

EXERCISE 1.1: Making a Grudge Inventory

GOAL   The goal of this exercise is to reflect on grudges that you're holding on to. This exercise is consistent with the fourth step of Alcoholics Anonymous, which involves conducting a moral inventory of yourself.

INSTRUCTIONS   List the grudges that you've collected related to your divorce. Start by writing down your grudges against your ex. Next to each grudge, rate the intensity of your anger on a scale ranging from 1 (minimal) to 10 (extreme). Once you've finished, make a list of grudges you're holding against other people, such as family members, attorneys, friends, or children. Use your journal or additional paper as needed.

If you're having a hard time identifying grudges—or believe that you aren't the type of person who holds grudges—focus instead on behaviors that you find annoying. When probed deeply, annoyances often reveal hidden pools of anger.

KEEP IN MIND   This exercise requires challenging self-reflection, particularly if you find it uncomfortable to acknowledge that you have grudges. However, once you recognize and name your grudges, you're in a better position to deal with them.

Name of Person	Grudge	Intensity (Scale of 1 to 10)

REFLECTION   Look back over your list and then answer these questions:

How long have you been holding on to these grudges?

_____

Did any of your grudges surprise you? If so, which ones?

_____

_____

_____

_____

Which grudge would be the hardest to let go of?

_____

Which grudge would be the easiest to let go of?

_____

Consider sharing your list or your answers to these questions with a therapist, close friend, or divorce support group. There's no need to be embarrassed about the fact that you have grudges. Who wouldn't have a few grudges after what you've been through?

Before moving on, we have to ask a question. Did you really do the exercise? C'mon, be honest! If you didn't write down your answers, we strongly urge you to do so now. Go ahead and mark up this book with your reflections. (And we're not just saying this so that your divorced friends will have to buy a brand new book without your writing in it.) Research has shown that writing down your thoughts and feelings can help you cope better with stressful events (Gortner, Rude, and Pennebaker 2006). Completing this exercise will help you become more aware of the role anger is playing in your life and will help you identify grudges that are easier to let go of when the time is right.

When Anger Becomes Automatic

"Just the sound of his voice makes my blood pressure rise." "I get pissed off whenever I see her new lover around town." "Every time I hear that song, it reminds me of his lies."

Can you relate to any of these statements? Anger can become so deeply ingrained over time that it becomes an automatic response. One factor that can play a role in this is *classical conditioning*. If you took an introductory psychology course, you'll recall that classical conditioning was discovered by a Russian scientist named Ivan Pavlov, who had a peculiar fascination with canine digestive systems. For those who didn't take introduction to psychology (or who slept through the course), we offer this brief refresher: Dogs reflexively begin to salivate when presented with food. However, Pavlov discovered that they also learn to salivate in response to objects that have been presented along with food, such as a bell or a light.

What do slobbering dogs have to do with your feelings toward your ex? Classical conditioning is one reason why it can be so hard to let go of anger. For instance, when you first met the person who later became your ex, the sound of his or her voice probably did not cause a negative emotional reaction (unless your ex had an unusually annoying voice). However, once that same voice became associated with hurtful words or actions, simply hearing it could elicit feelings of fear and anger. This association can endure long after the original transgression and sometimes takes place without conscious awareness. To get a sense of how automatic reactions might be influencing your attitude toward your ex, complete the next exercise.

EXERCISE 1.2: Finding Your Anger Triggers

GOAL   The goal of this exercise is to better understand how your automatic reactions are contributing to your anger.

INSTRUCTIONS   Think of memories, thoughts, characteristics, or experiences related to your ex that evoke automatic angry feelings in you. List these anger triggers in the space provided beneath the three examples.

ANGER TRIGGERS

Example 1: Hearing a song that reminds you of your ex.

Example 2: Seeing your ex around town.

Example 3: Driving by a restaurant or a bar that you and your ex used to frequent.

_____

_____

_____

_____

_____

_____

_____

_____

_____

_____

_____

REFLECTION   Count the number of automatic anger triggers that you identified. If you're experiencing automatic negative reactions in response to a large number of situations, classical conditioning might be an important component of your anger.

The bad news about classically conditioned feelings is that it can seem as though you have no control over them. The good news is that whatever has been learned can also be unlearned! Chapter 5 provides strategies for changing automatic anger triggers. Over the next few weeks, we encourage you to periodically review your anger trigger list as a means of gauging how your perspective is changing.

Being wronged or mistreated by your ex is like a spark that ignites a fire. By now, you probably have encountered plenty of sparks! Although your ex's hurtful actions provided the initial spark, fuel is needed to sustain a fire. Replaying the hurtful events in your mind can fuel your anger.

Sometimes fires can be useful. When camping, fires can be used for cooking, staying warm, and scaring away large, hairy, carnivorous beasts that might be lurking in the forest. (Sitting around a campfire may also lead to an irresistible urge to break out a guitar and start playing old John Denver songs.) Similar to fires, anger can have benefits.

Possible Benefits of Anger

Anger can serve as a signal of problems in a relationship. It can also motivate people to make important changes in their lives and to pursue justice. This point is particularly relevant for victims of domestic violence. One study found that women living in domestic-violence shelters who held on to their anger were less likely to indicate that they intended to return to their abusive partner (Gordon, Burton, and Porter 2004). If you have a pattern of remaining in abusive relationships, learning how to get in touch with your anger and channel it appropriately can be an important step toward healing. Becoming angry may enable you to move away, contact police, and seek out community resources for victims of domestic violence.

How Anger Contributes to Postdivorce Suffering

Although there can be benefits to getting angry, prolonged anger toward an ex in the absence of an immediate threat can cause suffering for you and those around you. Anger can keep painful experiences alive and can have a negative impact on your mental and physical health. If you have children, it can also have a negative impact on them.

KEEPING PAINFUL EXPERIENCES ALIVE

"Someone who gets angry about the things one should and with the people one should, and also as and when and for as long as one should, is praised," wrote Aristotle (2009, 50). If you ever meet a person like this, please let us know! Controlling anger is like managing a fire. If the winds change unexpectedly or too much fuel is added, it can turn into a raging inferno that is difficult to contain. Even after you succeed in dousing the flames, the embers can burn for a long time.

Judith Wallerstein (1986) tracked sixty divorcing families for ten years and found that about 40 percent of women and 30 percent of men reported high levels of anger toward their exes ten years after the divorce! Anger toward their exes persisted even though many of the participants had remarried. Interestingly, this study excluded high-conflict families that litigated custody or visitation issues. Had these high-conflict families been included, the percentage of very angry individuals probably would have been higher.

We read a news report about a particularly acrimonious court battle over a divorce settlement that lasted more than seventeen years. Remarkably, the legal battle lasted longer than the marriage. Surely after more than a decade any temporary benefits of feeling angry toward your ex have disappeared! Holding on to intense anger toward your ex can make it difficult to experience the peace and happiness that you're seeking, and can adversely affect your health.

ANGER AND PHYSICAL HEALTH

An ancient proverb states, "Before you embark on a journey of revenge, dig two graves." There appears to be scientific support for this idea. Consider these research findings:

- Hostility relates to coronary heart disease, and premature death (Smith et al. 2004).

- Individuals who spent twenty minutes recalling angry memories from their past showed more signs of physiological distress than when they were resting or recalling forgiveness memories for the same amount of time (Witvliet, Ludwig, and Vander Laan 2001).

The first finding is based on studies using correlational methodologies, which means it's not possible to determine whether hostility causes health problems or whether health problems make people more hostile. However, the second study employed an experimental methodology that allowed researchers to draw causal conclusions. If signs of physiological distress are apparent after a brief imagery exercise, imagine the possible ramifications of nursing grudges over many years! It turns out that grudges also relate to poorer mental health.

ANGER AND MENTAL HEALTH

Studies have shown that people with high levels of hostility are more likely to be depressed. For example, Stewart, Fitzgerald, and Kamarck (2010) tracked a group of healthy adults between the ages of fifty and seventy over a period of six years. Participants' hostile thoughts at the beginning of the study predicted depression six years later.

Why is there a relationship between hostility and depression? One possibility is that people often replay mistreatment in their minds over and over again. While this may initially help in making sense of what happened, it can also make you unhappy. Why allow unhappy experiences from the past to destroy your sense of peace in the present?

In addition to adversely impacting your own well-being after divorce, anger toward an ex can negatively impact others—especially your children, if you're a parent.

ANGER AND PARENTING

Without a doubt, co-parenting after divorce is tremendously challenging when there's a lot of acrimony between former spouses. Consider these two cases.

The Case of Ahmad

Ahmad, age forty-two, was married for thirteen years before divorcing. He has a daughter and a son, ages eleven and six. Ever since the divorce, his ex-wife, Debbie, criticizes his parenting skills in front of the children, despite the fact that he is a loving and competent parent. She undermines his parenting authority by insisting on picking up the kids from his home whenever they call to complain that their dad is disciplining them (for legitimately bad behavior). She also actively discourages the children from spending time with their father.

The Case of Isabella

Isabella, age thirty-three, has primary custody of her sons, ages four and seven. Her ex is supposed to visit the children every other weekend but rarely does. Time after time, he promises to call or spend time with them, only to leave them deeply disappointed by his failure to show up.

It's understandable why Ahmad and Isabella are deeply resentful toward their exes. Many divorced parents report that they can cope with their feelings when their ex treats them poorly, but that when their ex treats their children poorly, undermines their parenting, or actively tries to turn the children against them, their anger boils over. It's very difficult to keep anger toward an ex from affecting your children.

Often parents aren't aware of how their anger is affecting their children, however. They sometimes put their children in the middle of arguments without realizing it. Divorce expert Joan Kelly (2010) outlined several ways that parents put children in the middle following a divorce. Some of these are summarized in table 1.

TABLE 1: Five Common Ways Divorced Parents Place Children in the Middle

1. Demeaning your ex in front of the children
2. Asking children to deliver hostile messages to your ex
3. Encouraging children to keep information secret from your ex
4. Asking children to reveal intrusive personal information about your ex
5. Undermining your ex's parenting authority

Why are these actions such a problem? Because children who are caught in the middle between divorcing parents suffer deeply. Many children have deep connections with both their parents (even if their feelings are conflicted), and it's especially hard for them to cope when they are asked to choose sides.

Perhaps the best way to understand how ongoing parental conflict following divorce affects children is to listen to what they have to say. Charlotte Hardwick compiled letters that children of divorced parents wrote to a family judge into an interesting book called *Dear Judge*. If you have children and are going through a high-conflict divorce, you might want to read this book. The letters are insightful, poignant, and often heartbreaking. One of the letters is provided here:

Dear Judge,

-I don't want to carry any stupid messages back and forth.

-I don't want to pick a side.

-I don't want to hear any more bad things.

-I don't want to talk to any more child cycloigsts.

-I don't want to answer questions about the other house.

-I don't want to have to lie.

-I don't want to tell what the other one is saying.

-I don't want to have to say I like here better than there.

-I don't want a new dad or mom.

-I don't want to move.

-I don't want to keep any more secrets.

-I don't want to compare presents to the presents I get.

-I don't want to listen to any more arguments.

-I don't want to make excuses for my parents bad behavior.

-I don't want to lie to keep everyone happy.

-I don't want to always need my stuff that is at the other house.

-I don't want to explain why my parents act the way they do.

-I don't want to talk about it.

-I don't want to feel guilt, because I love them both.

Malachi O. (Hardwick 2002, 114; reprinted with permission)

Malachi is clearly unhappy with his circumstances and his parents' behavior. As a divorced parent, one of the best things you can do for your children is to engage in honest self-reflection about how your attitudes, feelings, and actions are affecting them. If you are a parent, we invite you to complete the next exercise.

EXERCISE 1.3: Reflecting on Postdivorce Parenting

GOAL   The goal of this two-part exercise is to reflect on your actions as a parent following your divorce.

KEEP IN MIND   This is one of the hardest exercises in the book to complete because it involves recognizing the possibility that, on occasion, your actions may have hurt your children. On the other hand, we also want you to think about ways that you have protected your kids from being hurt. So start there.

INSTRUCTIONS FOR PART A   List up to five actions that you have taken during the divorce that protected your children from unnecessary suffering.

Actions That Protected Your Children from Unnecessary Suffering
1.
2.
3.
4.
5.

REFLECTION   Take a moment to pat yourself on the back. The things you listed here are really important, and they have made a positive difference in the lives of your children. You should feel good about these things. Your children certainly do!

INSTRUCTIONS FOR PART B   Now comes the really hard part. List any actions that might have put your children in a difficult position following your divorce. This doesn't mean that you've intentionally done these things; you may have inadvertently placed your children in the middle. Don't forget that even really good parents sometimes make mistakes during a difficult and emotionally charged divorce. Your willingness to acknowledge mistakes takes courage.

Actions That Were Probably Not Helpful to Your Children
1.
2.
3.
4.
5.

REFLECTION   Sometimes parents feel deep sadness after acknowledging that their actions might have been hurtful to their children. Try not to be too hard on yourself! Everyone makes mistakes in tough situations. You did the best you could with what you had to work with at the time. The fact that you're taking the time now to consider these actions shows that you care deeply about how your actions affect your kids and that you want to learn how to make things better for them.

You might find it helpful to join a support group for other divorced parents so that you can talk with people who understand the tremendous parenting challenges you face and who will encourage you to give your kids the best chance of adapting and thriving after divorce.

This section tackled some of the ways that anger can negatively impact you and those you love following a divorce. Now it's time to turn your attention to another important negative emotion that's commonly experienced following divorce: sadness.

SADNESS AS A REACTION TO DIVORCE

A deep sense of loss following divorce is common because so many important aspects of life have changed. Cherished interpersonal relationships can be strained in unprecedented ways. Loss of companionship and intimacy combined with feelings of loneliness can be jarring. Having to leave a home in which you invested so much time and energy can make you feel like you're losing a part of yourself. Many people grieve over losing the dreams they once had for the relationship. Parenting often becomes more challenging, and there's nothing worse than not being able to see your children as often as you used to.

All of these losses can be hard to overcome and can contribute to feelings of sadness. If you're experiencing significant loss, know that you're not alone. And keep in mind that losses become magnified if you're trying to handle them on your own. This is the time to rely on those you trust and who care deeply about you. You may choose to reach out to a friend, a family member, a counselor, or a support group. If you are religious, you might also rely on God or members of a religious community. If a source of comfort is not readily apparent to you, do an Internet search and find out what divorce support resources are available in your area.

People sometimes ignore or deny the losses they have experienced following a divorce. Denial might help temporarily because it allows you to focus on other things. But it's not a good long-term strategy, because unacknowledged losses can interfere with a sense of peace. So, it's worth spending some time reflecting on what you have lost.

EXERCISE 1.4: The Undesirable Pie

GOAL   The goal of this exercise is to reflect on the losses you have experienced because of your divorce.

KEEP IN MIND   This exercise can be difficult, so we suggest picking a day and time when you're feeling mentally tough.

If you're depressed, we recommend that you wait to complete this exercise until your mood starts to improve. Also, you might want to hold off until you have a source of support, such as a close friend, therapist, or group with whom you can discuss your responses.

INSTRUCTIONS FOR PART A In this exercise, you'll make a pie graph to illustrate the losses that you've experienced. For those of you who enjoy baking or making cool pie graphs, this exercise is for you!

First, think of your least favorite type of pie. (For instance, we believe that putting spinach in pies is an affront to pie lovers everywhere.) Now imagine that this undesirable pie represents all of the losses you've experienced related to your divorce.

Take a moment to consider the individual losses—or slices—that make up the pie, and list them in the space provided.

Things You've Lost:

_____

_____

_____

_____

_____

_____

_____

_____

_____

_____

_____

_____

_____

INSTRUCTIONS FOR PART B   Now that you've identified your losses, use a pencil to draw slices on the pie (illustrated here) to represent how deeply each of the losses has affected you. Larger slices should be reserved for particularly painful losses, such as not seeing your children as often as you did before the divorce. Smaller slices should be reserved for less painful losses (such as no longer having someone around to kill spiders). Label each slice with the type of loss that it represents.

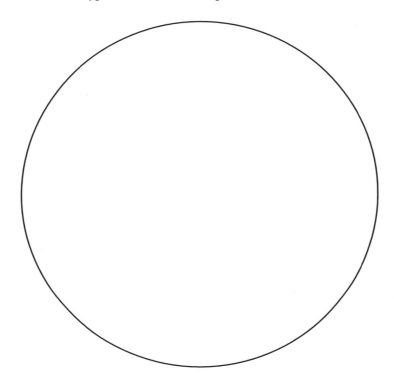

REFLECTION   Make sure you take some time to grieve over your losses. It doesn't hurt to have a good cry. Or two. Or three. Make sure you have a box of tissues nearby. Whether you're male or female, there's no shame in grieving. In fact—it's really important to get in touch with your sadness. As you go through the grieving process, try to be compassionate toward yourself (see chapter 3 for more on self-compassion). You've been through a lot! Also, it's important to talk with someone you can trust and who will listen without being judgmental.

We encourage you to periodically return to this exercise and redraw the lines on your pie graph as a way of documenting how your perspective is changing over time. As you learn how to apply positive psychology strategies to your life, we hope that some of the slices will shrink in size or disappear entirely.

It's completely normal for you to feel sad and down at times. Some even say divorce feels like someone close to them has died. But if your grief is debilitating for weeks on end and prevents you from engaging in your day-to-day activities, you may be suffering from depression. Learning how to spot symptoms of depression and knowing when to seek help are important skills to have following a divorce.

The Warning Signs of Depression

Unfortunately, depression is all too common, with almost one in ten people experiencing depression in any given year (Kessler et al. 2005). The causes of depression are complex and may include genetic influences, biological factors, thinking patterns, and stressful life events. Not everyone with depression experiences the same symptoms, which can differ from person to person in type, duration, frequency, and intensity. Some people experience recurring depression, with episodic bouts throughout their lifetime. Others have situational depression in response to a specific stressful event such as divorce. Regardless, depression is treatable and there's no need to suffer.

The next exercise contains a widely utilized depression screening instrument, the Patient Health Questionnaire (PHQ-9; Kroenke and Spitzer 2002). Keep in mind that a diagnosis of depression can be made only by a qualified mental health professional. However, we invite you to take the survey to familiarize yourself with the symptoms of depression and to help determine if you're at risk.

EXERCISE 1.5: Assessing Depression with the PHQ-9

GOAL: The goal of this exercise is to familiarize you with the symptoms of depression and to assess if you're at risk.

INSTRUCTIONS: Use a scale of 0 to 3 to answer how often the following problems have bothered you over the last two weeks (0 means not at all, 1 means several days, 2 means more than half the days, and 3 means nearly every day).

Over the last two weeks, how often have you been bothered by any of the following problems?	Not at all	Several days	More than half the days	Nearly every day
Little interest or pleasure in doing things	0	1	2	3
Feeling down, depressed, or hopeless	0	1	2	3
Trouble falling or staying asleep, or sleeping too much	0	1	2	3
Feeling tired or having little energy	0	1	2	3
Poor appetite or overeating	0	1	2	3
Feeling bad about yourself—or that you are a failure or have let yourself or your family down	0	1	2	3
Trouble concentrating on things, such as reading the newspaper or watching television	0	1	2	3
Moving or speaking so slowly that other people could have noticed. Or the opposite—being so fidgety or restless that you have been moving around a lot more than usual.	0	1	2	3
Thoughts that you would be better off dead, or of hurting yourself	0	1	2	3

To score, add up each column for a total score: _____ + _____ + _____ + _____

= _____ TOTAL SCORE

If you checked off any problems, how difficult have these problems made it for you to do your work, take care of things at home, or get along with other people? (Circle one.)

Not difficult at all   Somewhat difficult   Very difficult   Extremely difficult

Total Score Depression Severity (Kroenke and Spitzer 2002)

> 1–4 Minimal depression

> 5–9 Mild depression

> 10–14 Moderate depression

> 15–19 Moderately severe depression

> 20–27 Severe depression

REFLECTION: If you scored in the mild range, keep an eye on your mood. You may consider seeking professional help now or in the future. If you scored in the moderate or severe ranges, we strongly urge you to seek professional help.

If you're feeling depressed, it's hard enough to get through the day without the additional challenge of having to find and schedule an appointment with a mental health professional. You may need to reach out to a trusted friend or family member to help you with this process. Part of treating depression includes looking at and working to change certain thought patterns that are related to having a depressed mood. Regardless of your score on the PHQ-9, you may be susceptible to these negative ways of thinking.

Depressive Thought Patterns

Cognitive-behavioral therapists such as Aaron Beck (1979) noticed that people who are depressed tend to have negative thought patterns. Many of these thoughts are automatic, and people often aren't aware of them. Automatic thoughts can be hard to identify and a challenge to change. One common treatment technique for depression involves identifying these thought patterns and keeping a record of them, so you can discuss them with a therapist. What follows are some common patterns of thinking in depression (Burns 2000). You may recognize some of these ways of thinking in yourself.

All-or-nothing thinking. In all-or-nothing thinking, everything is black or white, and there's no room for shades of gray. For example, you see yourself as either successful or a complete failure—there's no in-between. This all-or-nothing thinking often emphasizes the worst in yourself and situations.

Personalization. Personalization involves believing you are personally responsible for things over which you have no control. For example, Sally's ex-husband has a drinking problem, and she blames herself for his alcoholism. She thinks, *If only I'd been a more supportive wife, he wouldn't have starting drinking so much.*

Overgeneralization. When people overgeneralize, they tend to make sweeping conclusions that go far beyond what is happening in the present. For example, you may think, *I'm depressed now. I'll always be depressed.*

Mind reading. Mind reading involves inferring what someone is thinking from their behavior. These inferences are generally negative. For example, John is in a bad mood when he comes home, so his partner thinks he must be mad at her. She doesn't consider that John could have had a bad day or that someone else might have gotten under his skin.

Must-statements. *Must-statements* involve having expectations about how people (including yourself) must behave. Psychologist Albert Ellis called this "musterbation." In a televised interview (1988), Ellis said, "The three main musts are 'I must do well or I'm no good,' 'You, you louse, must treat me well, or you're worthless and deserve to roast in hell,' and 'The world must give me exactly what I want, precisely what I want, or it's a horrible, awful place.'"

Magnifying and minimizing. When depressed, people often magnify the negative aspects of life and minimize their own strengths. For example, one may tend to make situations out to be worse than they really are while simultaneously downplaying internal and external coping resources.

Other depressive-thinking patterns. Other patterns include mental filtering (focusing on one or two negative details while discounting the wider picture), fortune-telling (predicting negative events for the future), and catastrophizing (emphasizing and expecting the worst possible outcome).

If you recognize any of these thought patterns as your own, good work! The first step is to notice them. With a qualified mental health professional, you can begin to identify even more of these thought patterns that contribute to suffering.

A sense of profound loss following a divorce is often accompanied by anxiety about the future. Anxiety is another reaction to divorce that can impact your postdivorce adjustment.

ANXIETY AS A REACTION TO DIVORCE

Because so many aspects of your life change after a divorce, it's not surprising if you're worried about what the future holds. Divorce can feel like you've been plucked from your familiar surroundings by a giant crane and dropped into a new and completely unfamiliar location. You're suddenly faced with the task of creating a new life and a new routine in the midst of considerable uncertainty.

Do you ever find yourself imagining the worst possible scenario that could unfold? Many of us entertain catastrophic scenarios in our minds, even though they are highly unlikely to occur. Toward the end of his life, Mark Twain reportedly said, "I am an old man and have known a great many troubles, but most of them never happened." Twain realized that people often subject themselves to needless worry.

Granted, some of the things people worry about following a divorce can occur. For example, your financial standing can change considerably after a divorce, and you may end up wondering how you're going to make ends meet; bills need to be paid and mouths need to be fed, regardless of the turmoil that is unfolding in your personal life. Some people worry about what it'll be like to live alone. Everyone who is going through a divorce has a unique set of anxieties based upon their past experiences and the circumstances surrounding their divorce.

Writing your anxieties down can help you step back and examine them with greater clarity than when they're simply spinning around in your mind. The next exercise invites you to reflect on any anxieties that you're experiencing related to your divorce.

EXERCISE 1.6: Watching Your Worry

GOAL   The goal of this exercise is to increase awareness of your worries.

INSTRUCTIONS   Make a list of the things related to your divorce that you've been worrying about. Try to list all of your worries, regardless of how large or small your concerns seem to be.

After you've finished, go through each item on the list and use a checkmark to indicate whether the thing you are worried about is mostly or completely within your control or mostly or completely outside of your control.

What You're Worried About	Outcome Is Mostly or Completely Within Your Control	Outcome Is Mostly or Completely Outside of Your Control

REFLECTION   Look back over your list and ask yourself the following questions.

How often do you find yourself worrying about the things you listed?

_____ once in a while

_____ regularly

_____ almost all of the time

What physical symptoms or health problems, if any, are you experiencing as a result of your worrying?

_____

_____

_____

Which of the following is true for you?

_____ *I never worry about things I can't control.*

_____ *I sometimes worry about things I can't control.*

_____ *I frequently worry about things I can't control.*

Many of us tend to worry about things that are outside of our control. Developing a greater awareness of when you are doing this is an important step toward overcoming the worry bug.

———————————————————————————

If you're experiencing a lot of anxiety, and it's affecting your mood and health, consider seeking professional assistance. Fortunately, there are effective techniques for helping folks manage their anxieties, and a skilled therapist can help you. It can also be beneficial to discuss your fears with friends or members of a divorce support group who've been down the same road. The bottom line is that you don't have to face your fears by yourself.

This is a challenging time, and it's no wonder if you're worried about your ability to cope. However, having doubts about your ability to cope is not the same as lacking that ability. Is it possible that you're underestimating your inner strength and resiliency? Are you willing to work on developing new ways of thinking and acting that can help you on your journey toward healing?

SUMMARIZING YOUR CURRENT EMOTIONAL STATE

Many folks find that anger, sadness, and anxiety related to their divorce can interfere with their ability to enjoy the present. When you carry these negative feelings into situations that have nothing to do with the divorce, it can seem like emotional baggage is weighing you down. The amount of baggage that each person carries depends upon a variety of factors, such as how you were treated by your ex, the level of conflict throughout the marriage and divorce proceedings, whether you have children, whether you have financial challenges, and your own style of handling stress. Table 2 contains three examples of how emotional baggage can affect people after a divorce.

TABLE 2: Emotional Baggage and Divorce

Examples	Baggage Assessment	Description
Example 1	*I'm traveling light.*	*I have some lingering hurts from my divorce, but they aren't interfering with my ability to move forward. I periodically think about these hurts, but they aren't on my mind on a daily basis. I'm traveling light and could fit my emotional baggage into a small backpack or a handbag.*
Example 2	*I'm packed and prepared for a long stay.*	*I feel burdened by emotional baggage from my divorce. It feels like I'm dragging a large, heavy suitcase behind me. Negative thoughts, feelings, and images related to my divorce occupy my mind on a regular basis. I wish someone could give me a hand with the load I'm pulling.*
Example 3	*I'm absolutely buried in baggage.*	*I'm carrying around so much emotional baggage from my divorce that I need to hire a small moving van to accompany me wherever I go. My family members and friends are having a hard time seeing the real me underneath this heavy load.*

Which of these examples do you relate to most? Regardless of the answer, be gentle with yourself. You didn't deserve to be treated the way that you were, and you handled it the best way that you knew how.

The good news is that no matter how much emotional baggage you're carrying around, you can choose how much of a load you want to carry from this point forward. Be assured that it's possible to travel without letting excess emotional baggage interfere with your enjoyment of the journey, and positive psychology strategies can help you do it.

At this point, you've reflected on your current emotional state and how your emotions are affecting you. We'd like to acknowledge how courageous this step was, particularly if you're hurting deeply right now. The process of honestly acknowledging your feelings, even ones that you're embarrassed about, is an important first step in the healing process. Becoming more mindful of the thought patterns and emotional burdens that you're carrying is a major step toward healing after a divorce.

Although divorce brings many emotional ups and downs, there are characteristics of the divorce roller coaster that should be comforting. To begin, the ride won't last forever—things will get better. This may be difficult to accept if you're depressed or at a low point emotionally right now, but it's true. Aaron Beck, the founder of cognitive therapy, observed that with depression, there's a tendency to believe that things will never get better. "Depressed patients have a special penchant for expecting future adversities and experiencing them as though they were happening in the present or had already occurred" (Beck 1979, 117). This way of thinking, of course, fuels the cycle of depression. Even when not depressed, none of us are very good at predicting how we're going to feel in the future (Gilbert 2006). So it's best to avoid making predictions about your future feelings based on your present negative feelings. Your negative predictions are often wrong, and they certainly won't help you feel better now.

Also, don't forget that there's more than one way to ride a roller coaster. Some folks experience a white-knuckle ride while others throw their arms in the air and draw on their inner strength to endure, overcome, and even thrive. An important factor in determining how you'll experience the ride is your perspective. Applying positive psychology techniques can transform your perspective and enable you to experience the divorce roller coaster in a powerful and life-affirming way.

WHAT'S NEXT?

Whew! This chapter has covered some intense stuff. This would be a good time to take a break before moving on. You may want to take time to stretch your legs, walk the dog, check your email, or grab a bite from the fridge.

The next step is to begin working on becoming more mindful in your daily life. Whenever you're ready, continue on to the next chapter.

CHAPTER 2

"Why Can't I Stop Thinking About It?"

Learning to Quiet Your Mind

Does it sometimes seem that your mind has a life of its own? Have you found that no matter how hard you try not to think about your divorce, troubling thoughts and feelings pummel you like waves beating against the shore? If so, we've got some bad news and some good news. The bad news is this is a common experience for many folks going through a divorce. Your mind just won't shut up. The good news is "you can't stop the waves, but you can learn how to surf," notes Jon Kabat-Zinn (2004, 30), the founder of mindfulness-based stress reduction. Consider Nina's case.

The Case of Nina

Nina has been separated from her husband Kurt for about two years, and they're in a nasty court battle over their divorce settlement. The primary reason for their divorce is Kurt's affair with Becky, one of his coworkers. Becky and Kurt moved in together not long after he separated from Nina, and understandably, Nina is hurt, angry, and embarrassed. Her emotions change from day to day, and sometimes even moment to moment. She finds herself lost in an inner monologue, obsessing about the reasons for the affair, whether she will be alone forever, and other troubling narratives. It's as if her mind were a music player on an endless loop, playing the same old songs over and over, and the stop button is broken.

One day, Nina took her two children to their favorite park, complete with the best jungle gym for miles around! It was early spring, the weather was beautiful, and they planned to spend time enjoying the sunshine. Unfortunately, Nina barely remembered the drive over because she couldn't stop thinking about the upcoming divorce hearing. Would Becky be there? What might the outcome of the hearing be? While at the park, the children kept asking her to play, but Nina became increasingly impatient. She really just wanted to be left alone to plan for the upcoming divorce hearing.

As a mother of two young children, newly single and trying to negotiate the painful and often traumatic divorce process, Nina is having a hard time finding peace of mind. When interacting with Kurt, her children, or other important people in her life, she finds herself reacting based on what is going on inside her head and not on what is occurring around her. Life is unfolding right in front of her, but she is missing it.

Feeling like you're at the mercy of your racing thoughts is a common experience for people going through a divorce. Fortunately, you can learn to accept and quiet your thoughts, which will enable you to respond more creatively and effectively to situations and help you achieve a greater sense of well-being. This can be accomplished through the practice of mindfulness, which is the topic of this chapter.

Chapter Focus

In this chapter, we define mindfulness, discuss why it can help you, and provide some suggestions for how to apply it to your day-to-day life as you work through the divorce process. The practice of mindfulness may be one of the most precious gifts you can give yourself!

WHAT IS MINDFULNESS?

Mindfulness is nonjudgmental awareness of your present moment-to-moment experience. It's a state of gentle, focused attention on things you may have previously ignored, including internal states (thoughts, feelings, body sensations) and external circumstances (physical surroundings, interactions with others).

The practice of mindfulness is centuries old and comes from contemplative spiritual practices found in both Eastern and Western religious traditions. You don't have to be religious or even consider yourself to be spiritual for this practice to improve your life. What's needed is a firm commitment to consistently repeat the techniques and perform them with an attitude of love and compassion toward yourself. When you're mindful, you're kind to yourself. You don't judge your perceptions or state of being. You just notice them and attempt to see them for what they are.

WHY BOTHER WITH MINDFULNESS?

Our minds tend to run off in directions that have little to do with our present experience, and when the going gets tough, we concoct elaborate *backstories*—some worthy of a Hollywood production! Your backstories are the narratives that go through your mind as you try to make sense of your experiences. These stories may or may not accurately reflect reality—they can be based on previous experience, expectations about the future, or personal bias—and depending on their content, they can increase negative feelings and make dealing with others more difficult.

The practice of mindfulness can counter your tendency to concoct backstories, but is it worth your time and effort? After all, navigating the divorce process already takes an enormous amount of time and attention. On top of all that, you must cope with the hassles of daily life. Based on the evidence, we think the practice of mindfulness is worth considering as a way to cultivate inner stillness and peace of mind, which can make this life transition easier for you and those you love. Practicing mindfulness may lead to several positive results.

Decreasing Rumination

Do you ever think about past events over and over again in your mind? *Rumination* is consistent, repetitive, and focused attention on past occurrences that produces negative emotions such as anxiety, hurt, shame, and regret. Like a cow chewing its cud, we chew on negative thoughts that keep coming up. Mindfulness is a technique you can use to decrease negative thought patterns and to recognize when those thought patterns are sweeping you away (Campbell et al. 2012; Jain et al. 2007). Through gentle awareness of your thoughts and feelings as they are occurring, their power is diminished. An often-used analogy likens the awareness of thoughts to touching a soap bubble. What happens when a soap bubble is touched? It pops and disappears. That doesn't mean that more bubbles or thoughts won't appear, but when those bubbles are touched by awareness, they lose their form.

Reducing Stress

Mindfulness doesn't make Nina's stressful upcoming divorce hearing go away, nor does it remove the pressures associated with being a single mother of two young children, but the practice does help her find a greater sense of peace and well-being. You might think of mindfulness as a subway strap that you hold on to when the ride gets rough. It doesn't change the nature of the ride, but the strap anchors and keeps you steady. When you're holding the strap (in other words, practicing mindfulness), you're less affected by the car's pitching and bumping. You're better able to look around and get a clearer picture of what's happening.

Over the past two decades, studies on mindfulness interventions have examined how this technique can enhance well-being among individuals with psychological disorders, medical problems, and everyday stressors. Some researchers use a type of study design called a meta-analysis, where they look at the results of several studies on the same topic to examine the consistency of the findings. One such study, conducted by Grossman et al. (2004), found that a mindfulness-based intervention helped people cope better with all sorts of conditions, including pain, cancer, heart disease, depression, and anxiety, and also enhanced the quality of life for people who didn't have a clinical problem.

Improving Relationships

The story of your former marriage is a complicated narrative filled with emotional hooks on which you easily can get snagged. Have you ever misinterpreted something your ex said or did because you were listening to that old narrative about your marriage playing in your head? Mindfulness can decrease relationship distress, enhance relationship satisfaction, and help you get more in tune with what others are trying to communicate (Carson et al. 2004). When you're mindful, you're also better able to see and understand the stressors that others are dealing with, which may help you have more empathy and compassion for them.

Promoting Clarity

Being aware of and noticing in a compassionate manner what you're thinking is key to mindfulness practice. Through this awareness comes clarity, and clarity gives you choices. When you're able to see things for what they really are, you can choose how you want to respond instead of automatically reacting to circumstances. When you're in a state of mindless rumination, your choices are limited because you react based on the content of your ruminations and the consuming emotions that result. When you're mindful, you see things more clearly as they're unfolding in the present, and you are less likely to be influenced by your mind's stories about the past or concerns about the future.

Clarity in the Midst of the Storm: The Snow Globe

Do you own a snow globe? If not, take a moment to picture a snow globe and what you would put in it.

Crystal's snow globe contains a little black dog, an ice cream stand, some tall trees, and a 1965 Ford Mustang. When the snow globe is shaken, it's difficult to see these objects, and important details are obscured, such as the breed of dog and type of Mustang. Similarly, when your life is shaken by divorce, thoughts swirl in your mind and difficult emotions cloud your vision. The more stressed you are, the bigger the resulting storm inside.

Once Crystal stops shaking her snow globe, she watches as the snow settles to the bottom, and then she can see that the Mustang is a fastback and that the little dog is a Boston terrier. Similarly, if you become still and pay close attention to your moment-to-moment experience, you can see more clearly what is going on in and around you. The cultivated stillness settles the snowstorm, and although the snow remains on the ground, it doesn't interfere with your ability to clearly see. This is how mindful, directed attention and awareness can lead to clarity.

CULTIVATING THE RIGHT ATTITUDES TO PROMOTE MINDFULNESS

According to Kabat-Zinn (2013), mindfulness is facilitated through the cultivation of seven interdependent attitudes. Developing and nurturing these attitudes will form a solid foundation for your mindfulness practice.

Being nonjudgmental. Your mind naturally categorizes and evaluates your experiences. By being an impartial observer of this activity, you're less likely to be swept away by this ongoing narrative. Therefore, mindfulness entails not judging your thoughts but just observing them. As you experience the myriad of emotions prompted by your divorce, your job is to compassionately notice what's going on both inside and around you by being fully present with what is unfolding moment by moment.

Patience. It's important to be patient with the divorce process and to learn to understand and accept that things unfold in their own time. When examining the activity of the mind, you accept that it will wander, but you don't get carried away by it. It does its thing, and you patiently watch and are open to what each moment brings.

Beginner's mind. Openness to new experiences following a divorce can be facilitated by cultivating a beginner's mind, the attitude that the old is new. It's a willingness to look at things with a fresh perspective, as if you are seeing them for the very first time. "In the beginner's mind there are many possibilities, but in the expert's there are few," says Zen master Shunryu Suzuki (2006, 1). This promotes receptivity to new experiences and prevents you from being stuck in preconceived notions.

Trusting yourself. You may not always understand why things happen as they do, but if you trust yourself as events unfold, you can find security in the face of instability. This is particularly true as you cope with the unexpected twists and turns that divorce can bring. Trust involves confidence and faith in your own wisdom and goodness, and it can lead to personal responsibility. Through nonjudgmental observation of your thoughts, feelings, and circumstances, you can learn to more fully trust your own experience, intuition, and authority, and to act in accordance with your own truth.

Nonstriving. When was the last time you were advised not to work hard? Contrary to the dictates of the surrounding goal-directed culture, mindfulness necessitates nonstriving, as there is really nothing else to do but be as present as possible. Comic Paul Dean once said, "The nice thing about meditation is that it makes doing nothing quite respectable." Mindfulness is being able to more fully experience what is already here. The only thing to do is just be, in the here and now, fully aware. This may be a comforting thought as you're going through your divorce.

Acceptance. Acceptance is a willingness to see things as they are without trying to change them. It doesn't mean condoning or approving of everything. Rather, it means making an openhearted effort to see things as they are without viewing life through the backstories your mind loves to tell. Acceptance is embracing what arises inside just as it is.

Letting go. The final attitude is letting go. Letting go entails seeing what is unfolding for what it is and then letting it fall away. You don't try to actively push unpleasant thoughts or feelings away, or cling to pleasant ones either. You look at them and then let them go. They will likely come back in one form or another, and you will need to let some things go, over and over and over again, countless times. We know you'll have ample opportunities to practice this during your divorce and its aftermath. That's where patience comes in, right?

LEARNING TO BECOME MORE MINDFUL

How do you apply mindfulness in your own life? In fact, there are many different approaches to mindfulness meditation, and we're not able to cover them all here. Our goal is to provide you with some basic techniques that can get you started in your mindfulness practice. We'll cover some strategies you can use to become more aware of your breath, body sensations, thoughts, and feelings so that you can inhabit each moment of your life more fully.

Your Breath Is Your Anchor

If you're alive, you're breathing. (Okay, that's obvious.) But while breath is your constant companion regardless of what's happening to or around you, this indispensable ally is often ignored. The breath provides you with your fundamental life rhythm and is with you until your physical body dies. With each in-breath, you are renewed; with each out-breath, you release and let go. The breath is a gauge for the state of both your physical self and emotional self. When you physically exert yourself or are emotionally upset, your breath becomes rapid or maybe even labored. With physical and emotional relaxation, it slows down and deepens. Sometimes your breath is shallow, other times slow and deep. In response to various life events, you may work to "catch your breath" or may experience something that can "take your breath away." In mindfulness practice, the breath is central and can be utilized as an anchor and stabilizer in times of stress. Take a moment to become mindful of your breath.

EXERCISE 2.1: Noticing Your Breath

GOAL   This goal of this exercise is to help you tune in to your breathing.

INSTRUCTIONS   After you finish reading these instructions, put the book down and sit for a moment or two observing your breath with your eyes softly closed. Then return to the book.

REFLECTION   What was that like for you? Did you notice your breath as it traveled through your nostrils? Did you feel your chest slowly moving up and down? Were you conscious of the breath on your upper lip as you inhaled and exhaled? Were you breathing deeply, or was the breath more on the shallow side? There are lots of other observations you can make. Who knew the breath was so interesting? Write down your observations in the space provided.

_____

_____

_____

When becoming mindful of the breath, remember that you're merely observing it. Although there may be times when you'll want to make the conscious decision to slow it down by taking deep breaths, for now try to become accustomed to just observing it. Don't analyze it. Don't evaluate it. Just breathe and see what unfolds moment by moment.

Increasing Your Field of Awareness

Mindfulness practice involves observing your thoughts, feelings, body sensations, and external stimuli. When stressed by life events, such as those experienced while navigating the divorce process, the body and mind can go into overdrive; you can experience uncomfortable body sensations and painful emotions and thoughts. And you are probably highly motivated to stop these hurts. But mindfulness teaches you that you don't have to distract yourself from these uncomfortable experiences. Through focusing compassionate awareness on these uncontrollable feelings or body sensations or thoughts, you learn that these experiences come and go, and they aren't static. The discomfort doesn't last forever—it goes away, and you survive.

It may help to think of awareness as the hub of a wheel, with the spokes extending from the hub to the wheel's rim representing awareness directed to various parts of the rim—which in turn represents your senses and the content of your mind (see figure 1). At any time, you can focus your awareness (via one or more of the spokes) to different parts of this rim of experience. For example, in exercise 2.1, you focused on the sensation of breathing, which is one of the many senses and experiences that make up the rim.

Figure 1: Wheel of Awareness

As you can see from the illustration, you can selectively focus your attention on various aspects of your internal and external experiences. One potential focus can be on your thoughts.

Paying Attention to Your Mind Chatter

Stress following divorce is often compounded by the incessant chatter that can run through your mind. Many divorced people focus on negative events that have occurred or worry obsessively about what will happen in the future. They try to push these troubling thoughts away, but to no avail, and they may beat themselves up for being unable to control what goes on in their own heads. It's as if telling yourself not to think about your situation is really an invitation to think more about the whole divorce mess!

In fact, research suggests that trying to suppress a thought—especially over long periods of time—produces even more thoughts of what you're trying not to think about.

In a classic study (Wegner et al. 1987), one group of participants was asked not to think about a white bear. Not surprisingly, they were unable to suppress thoughts about the white bear. This same group was later asked to think about the white bear. Their responses were compared with a group who was told from the very beginning of the experiment to think about a white bear. Those who were told not to think about a white bear reported thinking about a white bear more often than those in the other group! More research on this paradoxical effect of thought suppression demonstrates that people may be able to successfully suppress thoughts for a short period of time, but not in the long run (Abramowitz, Tolin, and Street 2001).

The human mind is constantly producing thoughts. Trying to stop your mind from wandering and thinking thoughts would be like trying to stop your eyes from making tears or your mouth from salivating (or your stomach from rumbling loudly during important meetings when you're hungry). Much of the time, your mind goes on its merry way, reveling in judgments, contemplations, ruminations, and obsessions, and you don't even realize this is happening. To stay anchored in the present, to respond to what is happening in the here and now, you must first become conscious of your mind chatter. (One therapist who worked with Crystal on mindfulness training called it "monkey chatter"—an apt description!)

Much of mind chatter takes the form of judgments or evaluations. For example, you may compare your experiences to similar experiences from the past and consider whether they meet or fall short of your expectations. These judgments are like a cloudy lens through which you perceive the events of your life. It's therefore difficult to see and fully experience the present moment.

Because mind chatter is often outside of your conscious awareness, the first step is to make a conscious effort to notice it—no easy task! If you're like most people, you really haven't considered your thoughts to be objects of attention, and the narrative that goes through your head just seems to happen. If this is true for you, don't expect that paying attention to your mind chatter will be easy from the outset. Examining the content of your thoughts takes work and diligence. Are you ready for the challenge?

EXERCISE 2.2: Getting in Touch with Your Thought Patterns

GOAL   This exercise is intended to help you get in the habit of monitoring your mind chatter.

INSTRUCTIONS   Take a moment to do a mind check. What thoughts are running through your mind? Don't censor yourself. Write down a few of your thoughts.

THOUGHTS

Example: *I'm thinking about all of the things I have to do today.*

_____

_____

_____

REFLECTION   How was that? Easy? Somewhat difficult? As you look at what you've written down, what types of thoughts did you have? Judgments, fantasies, worries? What you're going to have for dinner (Mark's favorite)? Or your tried-and-true monologue (or dialogue)? Please know that whatever you were thinking is just fine. Don't judge your thinking! The important thing is to notice it.

If that exercise went okay, we'd like you to write down what's going through your mind a few times each day, either using the following space in exercise 2.3 or writing in your journal. Because the process of becoming aware of your thought stream can be difficult, doing this exercise will get you in the habit of doing a mind check as you move forward. If, after the first day, you find that you're having a difficult time remembering to do your mind check, it may help to set up a reminder.

Some of our divorced clients have used the alarm function on their phones to remind them sporadically during the day. Others have worn a special bracelet or other piece of jewelry that they haven't often worn before; noticing it cues them to monitor their thoughts. Others have used sticky notes posted around their house or work space (it helps if you move them each day) as reminders.

EXERCISE 2.3: Monitoring Your Thoughts Throughout the Day

GOAL The goal of this exercise is to enhance your skill at monitoring your thoughts.

INSTRUCTIONS Over the next three days, write down what's going through your mind a few times per day. Please don't judge the content of your thoughts as good or bad, or acceptable or unacceptable. Simply observe your thoughts.

THOUGHT RECORD

Day 1/Date	What You Were Doing	What Was Going Through Your Mind

Day 2/Date	What You Were Doing	What Was Going Through Your Mind

Day 3/Date	What You Were Doing	What Was Going Through Your Mind

REFLECTION At the end of three days, what was this process like for you? Did monitoring your thoughts become more automatic over time? Did you need to rely on your reminders?

_____

_____

_____

_____

What did you notice about the content of your thoughts? How much of your internal narrative is related to your divorce? Did you discover anything surprising?

_____

_____

_____

_____

Did you notice any connection between what you were doing or the time of day and what was running through your mind?

_____

_____

_____

_____

Congratulations! You're making progress on your mindfulness journey. By gently examining what goes on in your mind throughout the day, you can better understand your internal life and how this connects with what happens in your external world.

You may have noticed yourself having certain repetitive themes among your thoughts. In Nina's story, we used the analogy of such themes being like a music player that plays the same songs over and over again, whether or not you want to listen to them. Does this resonate with you? If so, what songs does your mind player repeat? One of Crystal's clients used to play the song "If only I would have…" over and over. Take a moment to reflect on those old tired tunes that get too much play in your head. What would their titles be? In other words, what are the themes that get the most play on your internal listening device?

EXERCISE 2.4: Your Internal Thought Playlist

GOAL   This exercise will help you get in touch with the content of your mind chatter by paying attention to the prominent themes from your internal playlist.

INSTRUCTION   Write down a couple of song titles that reflect the thoughts that run through your head repeatedly. They could be borrowed from real songs or could be ones that you make up entirely on your own. Be creative!

PLAYLIST

List the titles of the songs on your internal playlist.

Song 1 _____

Song 2 _____

Song 3 _____

Song 4 _____

REFLECTION What themes do you notice? What seems to take up the most airtime for you?

_____

_____

_____

_____

_____

As you name and examine these tired themes, they tend to lose their power and letting them go becomes easier. You've likely held on to these themes for a long time, and you may find that you need to let them go over and over again. That's okay—it's just part of the process!

DEVELOPING YOUR OWN MINDFULNESS MEDITATION PRACTICE

Like most valuable skills, learning how to become more mindful requires dedication. In this section, we present a brief introduction on how to start a formal meditation practice. Formal practice merely sets the stage for engaging in mindfulness in day-to-day life.

Several years ago, Crystal gave into her curiosity about meditation and attended a free class at a local meditation center. There were about thirty people gathered in the room, sitting on chairs and cushions scattered on the floor. Incense was burning and Asian art adorned the walls. The leader, a thin man in his thirties, sat cross-legged on a cushion in the front of the group. He explained that he was going to lead the group in a meditation, discussed the reasoning behind the various components of the practice, and asked folks to share why they were there. Crystal, who is not one to be shy, immediately raised her hand and said, "I'm here because I want my mind to shut up. I want to be able to have a mental vacation once in a while. I want to think about nothing." The leader graciously smiled. He shared that there were many forms of meditation and that the form he was going to lead—vipassana meditation—was a noticing meditation. Instead of seeking to make their minds blank, participants were instructed to gently notice what was going on in their minds. And in doing so, paradoxically, their minds would begin to calm. Well, during that first formal meditation (which lasted over an hour), Crystal's mind was racing, her foot fell asleep, she had a crick in her neck, and an enormous kamikaze fly kept dive-bombing her ear. She left feeling discouraged and worried that she hadn't done it the right way. It would be quite a while before she gave meditation another try.

Crystal held common misconceptions about meditation. Although meditation has many forms, it's not about making your mind blank, but instead about becoming aware of what's present. Doing meditation is like taking a moment to look up at the sky. You can go for days without even noticing the sky or looking up at it. But, when you stop to look, you may notice all kinds of interesting things that go by, like beautiful clouds, birds, a blimp, or UFOs. The objects that cross the sky are like the contents of the mind: thoughts, feelings, body sensations, sounds, the rhythm of your breath—all of which come and go, often without your conscious awareness. But as you are meditating, you become aware of them and just watch them go by. The trick is not to get carried away by what you observe.

Crystal was happy to learn that there is no good or bad meditation—the experience you have while meditating is the experience you have. She also learned that meditating for over an hour the first time you try it is like running a marathon after spending a lot of time sitting on the couch eating donuts and watching *Seinfeld* reruns. It's wise to begin your mindfulness meditation practice gradually and work up to longer meditation periods.

Start gradually. Start with just a few minutes each day, and slowly work up to twenty minutes or more. You'll want to set aside at least ten minutes where you won't be interrupted by the phone, your children, or anything else. Many people meditate in the morning, before the rest of the household gets up; some prefer to do it right before bed, and yet others do it during the day when they won't be disturbed. Although you can lie down while meditating, we recommend sitting meditation at first—you want to fall awake, not asleep! Here is an exercise to get you started. Although we see so many benefits to regular meditation practice, try it out and see for yourself. Make a commitment to meditate regularly for a couple of weeks, and then make up your own mind about its benefits.

EXERCISE 2.5: An Introduction to Sitting Meditation

GOAL   The goal of this exercise is to introduce you to sitting meditation.

INSTRUCTIONS   Over the next week, set aside at least ten minutes each day to meditate in a place where you can do so without being disturbed.

If you can, sit on a cushion or a pillow on the floor either cross-legged or in a kneeling posture with the cushion or pillow between your feet. If you aren't able to sit on the floor, you can sit up straight in a chair and place your feet on the floor.

Set your timer for ten minutes. (Cell phones work great for this, as long as you're not taking any calls or texts.)

Make sure that your spine is erect and your shoulders are back but relaxed. Posture is important. You want to adopt a dignified posture where your back, neck, and head are vertically aligned and your hands placed comfortably in your lap or on your knees.

Now focus on your breath. Recall exercise 2.1, in which you observed your in-breaths and out-breaths and all of the things that you could notice. Thich Nhat Hahn (1991), a Zen master, suggests a technique to help focus on the breath: As you breathe in, repeat silently, "Breathing in, I know that I am breathing in." When you breathe out, say in your mind, "Breathing out, I know that I am breathing out" (8). This unites the body and mind.

It's okay if your mind wanders. That's what it does. When it goes off somewhere, just gently and firmly bring your attention back to the breath. You'll have to do this many, many times during a ten-minute meditation. That's perfectly fine. You are training yourself to be more fully present in the moment, and that's a process that takes time and patience.

If you need to shift your physical position, that's fine as well. Just do it mindfully. Pay attention to your body in space and your body as a whole as you move it.

REFLECTION: After doing your sitting meditation each day, write a few sentences about your experience. What did you learn about yourself? What was easy? What was difficult? Include any other observations you would like to make about the experience.

If you're seeing a therapist or are part of a support group, share some of your observations with others. What have their experiences with sitting meditation been like?

DAY 1	
DAY 2	
DAY 3	
DAY 4	
DAY 5	

If you'd like, increase the time you are meditating during your second week to thirteen, fourteen, or fifteen minutes per day. See if you can get up to twenty minutes. You may be thinking, *Twenty minutes? Are they out of their minds? How am I going to fit that in between walking the dog, working all day, scrounging up dinner, paying the bills, checking on Mom, and playing Words with Friends?* Some of us are really good at taking care of the needs of others and not so good about taking care of our own needs. By devoting this time to taking care of your well-being, you are being kind and loving to yourself. You are giving yourself the message that no matter how crazy things are, *I'm going to do something for me and I'm worth it.* The more mindful and peaceful you are, the better equipped you'll be to help those around you.

MINDFULNESS IN INTERPERSONAL RELATIONSHIPS

You can apply mindfulness skills to become more attentive to your interpersonal relationships. If you can commit yourself to being mindful of both what's going on inside you and what's happening with the people around you, it's more likely that you'll slow down and pause before responding when emotions and stress are running high. This can come in handy when co-parenting or dealing with your ex-spouse! This doesn't mean that you will never feel anger, frustration, disappointment, or any other negative emotion when interacting with others, but you can learn to be more receptive to these feelings and just notice them and let them go instead of avoiding or holding on to them.

Given that you are surfing the tumultuous waters of divorce, we bet that before long you will have an emotionally charged interaction with someone related to your divorce—your ex, your children, your attorney, or anyone else. So, next time you're interacting with people in your life that could play a role in an Oscar-worthy drama, take note and use it as an opportunity to practice mindfulness. The next exercise will help you become mindful of your experiences.

EXERCISE 2.6: The Influence of the Backstory on Your Thoughts, Feelings, and Body

GOAL   The goal of this exercise is to better understanding the impact of your backstories (the elaborate stories you concoct about situations) on your ability to see things as they are and to notice what is presently unfolding.

INSTRUCTIONS   The next time you have an emotionally charged interaction with one of the people connected to your divorce, complete this exercise.

During the interaction, notice your thoughts. What feelings are coming up? How is your body reacting? Look deeply. Don't avoid any unpleasantness or try to change anything, but just pay attention to what's happening as it unfolds.

Do what you can to let go of your backstory—you'll probably have to do this over and over—and to look at the other person through beginner's eyes. Listen to what the other person is saying as if you've never heard him or her speak before. Watch their body language as if you were meeting for the first time. If you find yourself getting emotionally reactive, just notice it: *I'm feeling anger,* or *Oh, that's frustration.* And before you reply to the person, pause briefly and choose how you would like to respond.

Mindfully respond to this person.

Do all of this compassionately.

KEEP IN MIND   Your response may not have been ideal. That's okay. Observe your thoughts about it. Remember, this is an opportunity to practice external mindfulness. (If you could do this perfectly, it wouldn't be called practice, would it?) Don't use this exercise as an excuse to beat yourself up because you aren't doing it right. We are asking only that you notice what is happening both internally and externally in a gentle, compassionate way.

REFLECTION   Briefly describe the situation and the backstory.

_____

_____

_____

_____

Describe your feelings as you observed them in the moment.

_____

_____

_____

_____

How was your body reacting?

_____

_____

_____

_____

What was it like being in the moment with this person?

_____

_____

_____

_____

How did you respond to this person? Did you feel you had a choice in how you could respond? Why or why not?

_____

_____

_____

_____

_____

Learning to listen mindfully to others has the potential to transform your interpersonal interactions. Look for other opportunities throughout the week to employ mindful listening, and see if you can begin to make mindfulness a way of life.

MINDFULNESS AS A WAY OF LIFE

Nondoing and just being for a few minutes per day can strengthen your mindfulness muscle for day-to-day living. It will provide you with a stable foundation that can help you live your life more fully and see what it has to offer as it unfolds moment by moment. If you think about it, that's all any of us have—what is right here, right now. As Mother Teresa said, "Yesterday is gone. Tomorrow has not yet come. We only have today."

The past has happened, and your recollections or regrets are merely thoughts, emotions, or memories of what has already occurred. The future has yet to come, and your compulsive planning or obsessive worries about it are also just thoughts that cross the sky of your awareness. You can't control the future. What is real is what you have right in front of you. If you aren't careful, the little monkey in your head could hijack the unfolding of your life.

We know that it's very difficult to be constantly mindful of your moment-by-moment experience, but the more you practice, the more those moments of clarity and full presence will begin to multiply. If the experience is positive, you don't have to cling to it. If it is negative or painful, you don't have to avoid it. You notice it, experience it, and then let it go. If you do dwell on it, you notice that and let those thoughts go too. And then you can choose. What a precious gift!

WHAT'S NEXT?

Now that you have the basis for living more mindfully, we're going to encourage you to cultivate a sense of self-compassion as you traverse the rocky terrain of divorce. Self-compassion can not only promote a peaceful state of mind but also help you connect better with others.

CHAPTER 3

"Why Can't I Cope with This Better?"

Developing Self-Compassion

Do you have an inner voice that always has a lot to say after you've made a mistake or perhaps acted less than perfectly? The one that goes on and on pointing out all of your misdeeds and character flaws? Who does this voice remind you of? Simon Cowell from *American Idol*? Your hypercritical parent? That cranky teacher you had in high school? Many of us have to contend with a resident inner critic who has plenty to say about who we are and what we do. Going through a divorce sets the stage for that faultfinder to go into overdrive—and as a result, you may feel inadequate, depressed, anxious, or all of the above. How can you relate to yourself in a healthier way when faced with your all-too-imperfect humanness? Self-compassion can help you cope with your inner critic.

The Case of Mike

His dad's words kept running through Mike's mind: *People in our family don't get divorced! There's got to be something wrong with you, Mike. Apparently, you don't have what it takes to make a marriage work.* Mike had figured his father would respond critically to the news that Mike and his wife, Danielle, had started divorce proceedings. Nevertheless, listening to his dad's rant had made Mike feel about twelve years old. It reminded him of the same tirade he'd heard when he told his dad he was quitting the summer football league. It was the same message: "You don't measure up—you aren't good enough."

Mike reflected on what his dad had said: *I suppose he's right: something is wrong with me. I'll be the first in the family to get a divorce. No matter what I did, I couldn't get things to work with Danielle. What a loser I've turned out to be.*

Truth be told, Mike asked Danielle to go with him to counseling many times, but she refused. Over the course of their marriage, he became increasingly concerned about her tendency to become emotionally distant and her unwillingness to communicate about what they needed to work on as a couple. Mike wanted reassurance and approval. He tried to make things right with Danielle, but he has a selective memory about how events unfolded. Unfortunately, Mike sees the breakup as his personal failure. Now Mike feels considerable shame about the divorce and can't believe that anyone has suffered as much as he has over the past eight months. Usually an outgoing person who enjoys his friends, Mike is becoming increasingly isolated and spends a good portion of his free time watching TV or playing video games by himself. His mind is preoccupied with replaying the past as he tries to better understand what he did wrong to cause this mess. If Mike's tendency to beat himself up emotionally were to manifest in physical bruises, he would be black and blue from head to toe.

Does any of this feel familiar to you? Mike's self-recriminating thought patterns are not only making his internal life miserable but also leading to behaviors that exacerbate the effects of his already stressful divorce process. For example, when he really needs to be surrounded by supportive people who care about him, he isolates himself. Instead of facing the emotions that have surfaced so he can move forward with his life, he chooses to distract himself. He's relating to himself during this difficult transition in a harsh and judgmental way—possibly the only way he knows. But you can learn how to walk a different route—you can take the self-compassionate path!

Chapter Focus

This chapter will help you explore the reasons why you may tend to be hard on yourself. We define self-compassion, discuss its benefits, and provide strategies for becoming more kind and loving to yourself as you cope with your divorce.

WHY ARE YOU SO HARD ON YOURSELF?

Many people struggle with an inner critic that rears its ugly head when circumstances are the most difficult. Unfortunately, this inner critic makes matters worse. Where does this critical voice come from?

Cultural and Familial Messages

We can imagine Mike's dad's response as we extol the benefits of being kind to yourself. "Self-compassion? Sounds like something for sissies and wimps!" His response isn't that unusual in society. Won't self-compassion make you soft and lazy? When you're hurting, aren't you supposed to "buck up," "walk it off, big guy [or gal]" or "grin and bear it," while repeating the mantra, "Tough times don't last, but tough people do"?

The messages received from the larger culture fortify the internal critics in all of us. Furthermore, many of us were raised in families where criticism was not a path to improvement—it was a sport. The impact of your parents or other important caregivers on your self-talk is significant. You internalize their criticism—its content, tone, timing, frequency—as a working model for how you treat yourself. These working models, called *schemas*, can determine if you're likely to relate to yourself with kindness or disdain. Growing up, Mike internalized his father's relentless criticism, resulting in self-talk that often focused on his inability to measure up to some ideal. How about you? As you think about your divorce, what messages does your inner critic consistently harp on? Where do you think those messages come from?

EXERCISE 3.1: Getting in Touch with Your Inner Critic

GOAL   The goal of this exercise is to increase your awareness of your critical self-talk related to your divorce and to explore the origin of these ideas.

INSTRUCTIONS   As you reflect back on mistakes you may have made while married or during the divorce process, think about the judgmental messages you give yourself. You may be able to quickly identify some of those messages, but, given their automatic nature, you may need to monitor this over the next couple of days and record others as they come up.

KEEP IN MIND   Remember, you're trying to bring awareness to the tone and content of your self-talk. Don't beat yourself up for beating yourself up in the first place! Try to bring nonjudgmental and loving attention to these messages. Don't think about the origin of these messages as fodder for your grudge list. Your caregivers most likely did the best they could in raising you—and remember, they were influenced by the messages they received from others too.

Content of Critical Self-Talk

Critical message 1: _____

_____

Where did this message come from? _____

Critical message 2: _____

_____

Where did this message come from? _____

Critical message 3: _____

_____

Where did this message come from? _____

REFLECTION   What themes emerge from these messages? For example, are they focused on self-doubt, self-rejection, self-pity, self-blame, or some other theme?

_____

_____

What's the most common source of your critical self-talk? In other words, where did most of these messages come from?

_____

_____

What emotions do you feel when you engage in this type of self-talk?

_____

_____

_____

Taking a good, honest look at the self-inflicted criticism that runs through your mind is not easy, so you should congratulate yourself for doing this. Again, the purpose is not to blame others for what you're thinking, but to better understand what aspects of your self-talk need compassionate attention as you move forward.

However, family and cultural messages are not the only explanation for why you may be hard on yourself.

Negativity Bias

Have you ever gone through a job evaluation at work? Has someone ever given you feedback about something you did, like a performance or a speech? Can you think of other times when you've been formally evaluated? Now think about the feedback you received. We bet you a hot fudge sundae that you first recalled the negative feedback you received, even if it was only a small proportion of the total feedback provided. Turns out, this is how the brain often works, typically giving more weight to negative versus positive information.

This effect has been demonstrated in the laboratory. Ito et al. (1998) showed positive, negative, and neutral pictures to college students while monitoring the electrical activity of their brains. They found that participants' brains were more active in response to positive and negative images than in response to neutral images. But when participants viewed positive and negative images only, the researchers found a negativity bias—the participants' brains responded more strongly to the negative images.

The researchers theorized that the negativity bias might have evolutionary origins and adaptive advantages under certain circumstances. For example, it would make more sense for you to notice and pay attention to that pissed-off two-ton rhinoceros bearing down on you than to look instead at the beautiful, serene waterfall that also happens to be in your field of vision. But this vestige of prehistory isn't always helpful in modern life. Negative messages get your attention, have more weight, and, depending on their source and timing, are likely to be internalized—whether or not they are true. Understanding how your mind works can be a step toward developing more compassion for yourself.

Protective Function

Interestingly, being hard on yourself may serve a protective function. We both teach college classes—Mark in psychology and Crystal in social work. At the end of every semester, the students evaluate our classes. Their evaluations help us understand how to better serve our students, and they also impact our career advancement. Before opening the dreaded manila envelope containing the evaluations, Crystal usually thinks about all the things that went wrong over the course of the semester and, of course, about how she isn't as good a teacher as others at the college. But when she reads her evaluations, she generally finds they are pretty good—except for the few students who felt she graded too hard or thought the readings were dry. When Mark opens the envelope, he focuses too much on the occasional critical comment and not enough on the many positive comments.

So why the self-flagellation? Being negative may serve a protective function: it's like you're giving yourself a preemptive beating, getting in some good licks before anyone else can. By taking a defensive posture, you're steeling yourself for the blows to come—that way they won't hurt as much. Paradoxically, this attempt to feel better, over the long run, can make you suffer even more. So how can you deal with these predisposed ways of thinking about yourself? Self-compassion may hold some answers. But before we get into what self-compassion is, we want to make sure you know what it isn't.

DEVELOPING SELF-COMPASSION

WHAT SELF-COMPASSION ISN'T

We've all thrown a pity party for ourselves at one time or another. You know the scene—all alone in the privacy of your mind, you ruminate on disappointments and problems and, for good measure, throw in a little exaggeration to ensure that no one could possibly have it worse. Although we all experience self-pity from time to time, ultimately it isolates us from others. Self-compassion, a kind and loving attitude toward the self, connects you to others. With self-compassion, you choose to acknowledge that other people have likely made the same mistake—you're not alone in your fallibility. This acknowledgment that others are in the same boat is not an excuse to gloss over or ignore your mistakes, but a loving attitude toward the self that can motivate you to do something different in the future. When you wallow in self-pity, you can get stuck in the pity pit.

Self-compassion is also different from self-esteem. Self-esteem is an evaluation of your worth as a person and tends to be the outcome, not the cause of, doing well in various pursuits (Baumeister et al. 2001). Over the past few decades, researchers and school systems have invested considerable resources in promoting self-esteem, but it's not a panacea. It's true that people with high self-esteem experience less anxiety, as well as greater well-being, than those with low self-esteem (Pyszczynski et al. 2004), but the pursuit of high self-esteem also has its costs. It can result in a tendency to focus on the things that you already do well and to avoid those that you don't, and to compare yourself to others in competitive ways that set you up for self-enhancement. As such, the pursuit of high self-esteem can be an obstacle to relating to others, learning, and self-regulation (Crocker and Park 2004). An alternative way of relating to the self, one that promotes clarity and doesn't involve self-judgment, is self-compassion. The next section discusses the three components of self-compassion and guides you through some exercises designed to explore this new way of connecting to yourself.

WHAT IS SELF-COMPASSION?

Kristin Neff (2003) is a psychologist who pioneered the scientific study of self-compassion. A concept that emerged from Buddhism and was secularized for wider application, her definition consists of three interdependent components: self-kindness, connection to other human beings, and mindfulness (introduced in chapter 2). Before getting into the nitty-gritty definition, here's a way to see how self-compassionate you are. The following exercise will help you look at how you behave toward yourself when times are difficult.

EXERCISE 3.2: How Self-Compassionate Are You?

GOAL   The goal of this exercise is to assess your current level of self-compassion.

INSTRUCTIONS   Take the following survey (reprinted from Raes et al. 2011) and calculate your scores.

PART A   For the first set of items, use the following scale:

how I typically act toward myself in difficult times

Please read each statement carefully before answering. To the right of each item in the box, indicate how often you behave in the stated manner, using the following scale:

Almost never				Almost always
1	2	3	4	5

I try to be understanding and patient toward those aspects of my personality I don't like.	
When something painful happens, I try to take a balanced view of the situation.	
I try to see my failings as part of the human condition.	
When I'm going through a very hard time, I give myself the caring and tenderness I need.	
When something upsets me, I try to keep my emotions in balance.	
When I feel inadequate in some way, I try to remind myself that feelings of inadequacy are shared by most people.	

PART B   For the next items, use the following scale (**note:** the endpoints of the scale differ from Part A):

how I typically act toward myself in difficult times

Please read each statement carefully before answering. To the right of each item in the box, indicate how often you behave in the stated manner, using the following scale:

Almost always				Almost never
1	2	3	4	5

When I fail at something important to me, I become consumed by feelings of inadequacy.	
When I'm feeling down, I tend to feel like most other people are probably happier than I am.	
When I fail at something that's important to me, I tend to feel alone in my failure.	
When I'm feeling down, I tend to obsess and fixate on everything that's wrong.	
I'm disapproving and judgmental about my own flaws and inadequacies.	
I'm intolerant and impatient toward those aspects of my personality I don't like.	

Total (sum of all 12 items) _____

Average score = Total/12 (take the total from above and divide it by 12) _____

    Average overall self-compassion scores tend to be around 3.0 on the 1–5 scale, so you can interpret your overall score accordingly. As a rough guide, a score of 1–2.5 for your overall self-compassion score indicates you are low in self-compassion, 2.5–3.5 indicates you are moderate, and 3.5–5.0 means you are high.

REFLECTION

Based on your score, how self-compassionate are you at this time?

_____

_____

Do you think this is an accurate reflection of how you treat yourself? Why or why not?

_____

_____

_____

Based on what you know so far about self-compassion, how do you think it might benefit you throughout the divorce process?

_____

_____

If you aren't as self-compassionate as you'd like to be, start working on that now by being kind to yourself about your lack of self-compassion! As previously discussed, being loving toward yourself may not come easily, given the messages to which you have been exposed. Here are the three components of self-compassion outlined by Neff (2003).

Self-Kindness

The opposite of self-kindness is self-judgment and blame. In exercise 3.1, you explored the messages of your inner critic—messages that can be harsh, judgmental, and downright mean. On the opposite side of the continuum, self-kindness is self-talk that is nurturing, gentle, and supportive. It's an understanding and tender way of being with yourself. When people are kind to themselves, they accept the fact that they aren't perfect, and when things go wrong, they actively comfort and soothe themselves rather than respond stoically or critically. Giving yourself understanding and love can help you feel worthy of acceptance and caring from others.

Connection with Humanity

Compassion can be defined as suffering with another person, feeling sorrow and deep sympathy for his or her misfortune, and having a strong desire to alleviate that suffering.

It comes from acknowledging that being imperfect is part of the human experience—that everyone makes mistakes, commits misdeeds, has mishaps, and suffers calamities. You can take that feeling of compassion that you so often feel for others in difficult situations and direct it toward yourself. When you barrage yourself with harsh and judgmental self-talk, you often make matters worse. You feel not only horrible about what has happened but also alone and isolated. But if you can be loving toward yourself, and acknowledge that others likely have experienced the same thing, you will feel less alone and more connected to others. This can help alleviate the severity of your distress.

Mindfulness

Mindfulness in the context of self-compassion is the same as we've discussed previously—an awareness of your present experience and a willingness to accept it as it is. When you're mindful, you neither avoid difficult emotions or parts of the self that you find unpleasant nor ruminate on them. Instead, you cultivate equanimity, a balanced awareness of the present moment and an ability to let things go. Equanimity provides calm within the storm, stability in the face of stress and tension. The practice of mindfulness avoids what Neff calls *overidentification* with painful emotions—a tendency to ruminate on the past or project into the future. Mindfulness helps you avoid getting caught up in the backstories your mind creates, allowing you to be open and fully present.

Putting It All Together

Considering these three components, self-compassion is a warm feeling of being fully human, connected to others, and healthy, instead of being driven by the need to be better, special, or perfect. This feeling underlies the relationship you have with yourself: whether you relate to yourself in a kind and gentle way or are critical and harsh with yourself. Self-compassion is a dynamic process that evolves over time, and the nature of that process will depend on your background, the strength of your inner critic, and the steps you take to change your inner life. If being kind to yourself seems like a foreign concept, that's okay. To become more comfortable with the idea, we invite you to imagine a *compassionate other*: a nonjudgmental person who is empathic, warm, and forgiving of your faults or mistakes. The following exercise is inspired by Gilbert (2009).

EXERCISE 3.3: Your Image of a Compassionate Other

GOAL   This goal of this exercise is to develop an image of a compassionate other.

INSTRUCTIONS   Think about a difficult situation related to your divorce. Do you have the situation in mind? For example, some people have a difficult time interacting with their ex face-to-face. When in this situation, they become flustered and say things they wish they hadn't said. Try to come up with your own example of an experience in which a little self-compassion would be helpful.

IMAGERY EXERCISE   Now, imagine that you wanted to share this experience with a kind, nonjudgmental, compassionate person who emanates empathy, warmth, and forgiveness—not to get advice or to solve the problem, but to be heard, comforted, and validated. Conjure up the image of this person with whom you'd like to talk. The image can be of a person you know, a composite of several people you know, someone you've heard of but don't know personally, a spiritual figure, or someone completely based in your imagination. It doesn't matter as long as the image works for you. Do you have the image now? Take a few deep breaths, center yourself, and connect with this person or being on a feeling level. Feel this person's love and acceptance.

The final step is imagining yourself talking to this person about this problem related to your divorce. Tell this compassionate other about what happened and absorb the response you receive.

REFLECTION   What qualities did your compassionate other possess? For example, warmth, kindness, openness? Describe the qualities of your compassionate other.

_____

_____

_____

_____

How did you feel as you talked to this person? For example, accepted, cared about, connected? Describe how you felt.

_____

_____

_____

_____

What kind words or phrases did your compassionate other express to you?

_____

_____

_____

You can use this image of a compassionate other whenever your inner critic gets on a roll. When you start to hear judgmental self-talk, invite your compassionate other in on the conversation. What would this compassionate other say in response?

WHY SHOULD YOU BOTHER WITH SELF-COMPASSION?

In this chapter, we're inviting you to change the nature of the relationship you have with yourself. We wouldn't encourage you to embark on such a journey without evidence that self-compassion may help with the challenges you're currently facing. One recent study concluded that self-compassion relates to emotional recovery after divorce.

Sbarra, Smith, and Mehl (2012) assessed the level of self-compassion exhibited by divorcing adults and then measured their degree of psychological adjustment to divorce. This study considered a number of variables, including relationship demographics, mood states, how people dealt with emotions, and attachment styles, to better understand the nature of the relationship between self-compassion and adjustment. Even when considering those other variables, the researchers found that those high in self-compassion had less divorce-related distress at the beginning of the study and up to nine months later.

Other scientific studies have found that self-compassion relates to better psychological health, more supportive relationships, and increased goal achievement.

Self-Compassion Relates to Better Psychological Health

Remember Mike from the beginning of this chapter? After he told his father about the breakup of his marriage, Mike responded to his dad's rant with harsh and demeaning self-talk. This sort of shame-based thinking can add fuel to the self-critic's fire.

However, when you're self-compassionate, that negative spiral can be prevented. Scholars are finding that people who are self-compassionate tend to cope better when under stress because they engage in positive cognitive restructuring (Allen and Leary 2010). In other words, relating kindly to yourself changes how you think about and process stressful events, which can decrease your tendency to ruminate and focus on the negative. Scientists are discovering that self-compassion may help to neutralize potentially toxic emotional states. People who are self-compassionate feel the pain associated with divorce, but unlike Mike, they don't make matters worse by punishing themselves with self-recrimination and rumination. Self-compassion appears to help circumvent these negative mental states. Furthermore, Neff and Germer (2013) found that people who took an eight-week self-compassion workshop showed greater decreases in depression and anxiety and greater increases in life satisfaction than those who didn't take the workshop.

Self-Compassion Relates to More Supportive Relationships

Interestingly, the more you're able to comfort and soothe yourself, the more good stuff you'll have to share with others. Neff and Beretvas (2012) found that high levels of self-compassion among heterosexual couples are associated with healthy relationship characteristics such as emotional warmth and acceptance of one's partner. Self-compassionate people also handle conflict in close relationships in a more balanced and healthy way (Yarnell and Neff 2013). Furthermore, when interacting with friends, self-compassionate people are more likely to be supportive than those who are low in self-compassion (Crocker and Canevello 2008).

Self-Compassion and Increased Goal Achievement

As a professor of social work, one of Crystal's pet peeves is grade grubbing among her students. She teaches young people the basics of clinical social work, and when faced with the question "Is this going to be on the test?" she's troubled. This question comes from the student's need to perform well, not from a desire to really learn the material. According to psychologist Carol Dweck (2006), *performance goals* (the fodder of the grade grubber) are related to approval and the maintenance of self-esteem. *Learning goals* are connected to trying hard at something because you find it inherently satisfying.

Guess which of these goals self-compassionate people are more likely to possess? That's right, it's the learning goals. Self-compassionate people are likely to directly confront their setbacks, work through them, and learn from their mistakes. They do this because they are motivated by what is best for them. Self-compassion comes from a place of love—you set goals and work toward them because you want well-being and happiness for yourself, not because you need to impress someone. Self-compassionate people have ambitious goals but experience less disappointment if things don't work out as planned.

Are You Convinced Yet?

So, do you think having more self-compassion for yourself related to your divorce sounds like a good idea? We hope so! To us, the evidence is strong that adopting a loving stance toward yourself when the going gets tough can be helpful. Building on the work you've done so far, the rest of this chapter concentrates on enhancing your self-compassion. Remember, this is a process. The snappy comebacks from your self-critic didn't develop overnight. Those jabs were likely honed over years of rumination and internalizing negative messages. Therefore, be patient with your attempts at self-compassion. With mindful diligence, you can develop a new and more loving relationship with yourself.

HOW TO DEVELOP SELF-COMPASSION AFTER DIVORCE

This section offers some practical ways to help you develop a more loving attitude toward yourself.

Practicing Self-Kindness

"When the going gets tough, the tough beat themselves up." Well, that's not exactly how the saying goes, but it's often what happens.

When you judge yourself harshly, you aren't being loving to yourself, but when you self-soothe, it becomes more difficult to berate yourself. Giving yourself a metaphorical hug can't be done while you're kicking your own butt! Psychologist Paul Gilbert (2009) points out that your emotional experiences stem in part from different physiological patterns triggered in your brain and body. Your body's reaction to self-soothing differs from its reaction to self-criticism. Kindness, tenderness, and warmth signal to your brain that you're safe and secure and can relax; cruelty and threats prompt fear and anxiety. Although all of these reactions are a natural part of the human experience, you may get stuck in patterns that keep the threat system activated. Self-compassion may be an antidote. "Kindness, gentleness, warmth, and compassion are like basic vitamins for our minds" (Gilbert 2009, 44). The next exercise explores how this might work.

EXERCISE 3.4: Activating Your Soothing System

GOAL This goal of this exercise is to find ways for you to quickly activate your self-soothing system, so you can beat your internal critic to the punch!

INSTRUCTIONS In exercise 3.3, you thought of a difficult situation related to your divorce. Going back to that experience, think about what you could have done to be more self-compassionate in the wake of that event.

QUESTIONS Going back to exercise 3.3, what did your compassionate other tell you about that situation? What are other compassionate words or phrases you might add? Begin a list here.

_____

_____

_____

_____

Now, develop a list of general self-compassionate statements that could work in other difficult situations related to your divorce. To help get you started, think about Mike from the beginning of the chapter. Here are some self-soothing statements that might work for Mike:

I am having a really hard time right now with what's going on with my divorce, and that's okay. Lots of people in my position would feel the same way.

It's no wonder I'm so tough on myself, given my family background.

I would accept someone else who was going through this. I want to accept myself, too.

It's not true that I am a loser. Although I have made mistakes in the past—and who hasn't?—I also do lots of things right.

Record some statements that would work for you. You can add to this list later as more ideas come to you. For now, try to come up with five self-compassionate statements.

1. _____

2. _____

3. _____

4. _____

5. _____

_____

Now you've got some self-soothing statements that resonate with you, which you can use during those difficult times that you'll inevitably face as part of living life—we all have those!

Realizing We're All Connected

When your self-critic is running amok, it can be easy to become self-absorbed and bogged down in feelings of insecurity and self-loathing. In that state, it's common to compare yourself to others, to make a case that you're the lowest form of life on the planet: *I've got to be the worst person ever. No one could be as bad as I am.* Or you may engage in upward comparisons and resent others in the process: *Bradley and Doug have such a perfect marriage. They get along great, their kids are angels, and they've got money. I'll never be that happy.* Either way, the result is a feeling of isolation that doesn't help you to move forward; it just keeps you stuck. Plain and simple—social comparison sets you apart.

One way to feel connected to others is to realize that fallibility is part of the human condition. We all have messed up before and will do so again. According to one review of the scientific literature on infidelity, at least one in five married people have an extra-marital affair at some point in their marriage (Campbell and Wright 2010). (And the list goes on and on—if it can be screwed up, human beings are up to the task!) Your self-critic may be quick to slap on a pejorative label setting you apart; Mike, for example, called himself a loser. Whatever the label, it distances you from others. The next exercise (adapted from Neff 2011) can help you lose those labels, so you can better realize your interconnectedness with others.

EXERCISE 3.5: Letting Go of Negative Labels

GOAL   The goal of this exercise is to help you identify traits you share with others, so you'll stop labeling yourself in a negative manner.

INSTRUCTIONS   You may label yourself as lazy, angry, or as a perfectionist—you may stick a lot of negative labels on yourself—but there are many other people who share the same characteristics. (Crystal often thinks of herself as bossy.) Choose one of these negative labels that's important to your self-definition—one that you beat yourself up about. With that label in mind, answer the following questions.

QUESTIONS   What is your negative label?

_____

How often do you display behavior that's consistent with that label? For example, all of the time, most of the time, some of the time? If you aren't acting in a way that reflects this label, are you still you?

_____

_____

When are you most likely to act this way? Are there times when you don't act this way? Does this label really define you if certain circumstances must be present for the behavior to emerge?

_____

_____

_____

_____

_____

Where did the trait or behavior that led to the label come from? What sort of causes and conditions led you to giving yourself this label? If outside forces are partially responsible for this label, what does that mean about its ability to define you?

_____

_____

_____

_____

_____

Who else do you know who wears the same label? Does this label define those people, or are they more than that?

_____

_____

_____

_____

_____

REFLECTION   "Being human is not about being any one particular way; it is about being as life creates you—with your own particular strengths and weaknesses, gifts and challenges, quirks, oddities" (Neff 2011, 79). With this in mind, how could this exercise change how you define yourself?

_____

_____

_____

_____

_____

_____

_____

The bottom line is that you're not alone in your feelings of inadequacy and insecurity. And though you might not be able to change those feelings, you can relate to these difficult emotions in a kinder way. That's where mindfulness comes in.

Practicing Mindful Self-Compassion

If you recall from chapter 2, mindfulness is the nonjudgmental awareness of your moment-to-moment experience. Mindfulness gives you an opportunity to be fully present and to see things as they really are. With mindfulness, you learn to accept your experiences and then let them go. You don't cling to pleasant emotions; nor do you avoid painful ones (which can in fact lead to suffering).

In their books on self-compassion, both Kristin Neff (2011) and Christopher Germer (2009) present a commonly used expression: _pain x resistance = suffering_. This equation indicates that your emotional suffering is directly related to your need for things to be different than they are. For example, you can feel hurt that members of your ex's family don't speak to you anymore, but the more you obsess about why or about how things could have been different if the ex hadn't been such a jerk, the deeper the hurt becomes. In other words, pain is inevitable; suffering is optional. If there is zero resistance, there is zero suffering. (We had to reach way back to high school math for that one!)

This resistance to painful emotions and circumstances often stems from a desire to control what is happening. A sense of control provides security, but unfortunately, many of life's twists and turns are beyond our control. That's why acceptance, letting go, and self-kindness are all part of the self-compassion recipe. Adding these ingredients helps us to avoid suffering.

EXERCISE 3.6: Embracing Your Pain to Avoid Suffering

GOAL The goal of this exercise is to help you become better at mindful self-compassion.

KEEP IN MIND As you do this exercise, remind yourself that many people have felt the same way you do under similar circumstances. And don't forget that emotional states don't last forever—you don't have to push them away, as they'll subside on their own.

INSTRUCTIONS Pay attention to your emotional landscape, particularly to difficult feelings triggered by your divorce. The next time you feel distressed about your divorce, take a moment to look at that emotion using the following process:

Approach your emotional state with a loving openness and curiosity. Tune into your breath and take a look at what's going on inside you. What are you feeling? What's prompting this reaction? Don't try to change it or wish it away.

Observe the emotion's intensity. Does it ebb and flow? Does it get stronger or weaker?

Use some of your self-soothing statements from exercise 3.4 to provide comfort to yourself.

REFLECTION How have you characteristically dealt with difficult emotions?

_____

_____

_____

_____

How was this experience different?

_____

_____

_____

_____

_____

_____

_____

CULTIVATING A SELF-COMPASSIONATE EXISTENCE

Way to stay the course on your self-compassionate path! Self-compassion is characterized by openheartedness and openmindedness. The kinder you are to yourself, the less defensive you will be as you interact with others. The more you can see your commonality with other human beings, the more empathy and understanding you can exhibit.

We'd like to end the chapter in the same way we started by reminding you to have compassion for yourself as you work on building your inner strength. Don't forget—everyone is a work in progress. As you navigate the stream of life, there are unexpected turns—as well as hidden waterfalls, beautiful rainbows, snapping turtles, funky forms of algae, and all sorts of surprising, scary, and wonderful things—along the way. Hopefully, you can learn to go with the flow and keep your maniacal upstream paddling to a minimum. Who says that what's upstream is any better than what is here right now, anyway? Sometimes the greatest personal growth comes in the midst of deepest suffering.

WHAT'S NEXT?

As we reminded you in this chapter, everyone makes mistakes. Sometimes, you can find yourself on the receiving end of another's harmful behavior, and you may have a hard time letting go of the hurt and anger you feel. Is forgiveness an appropriate response in such situations? The next chapter explores the nature of forgiveness and your willingness to consider it in your journey toward healing.

CHAPTER 4

"*These Feelings Are Weighing Me Down*"

But Are You Ready to Let Go?

I t's time to discuss the "f" word. The word we are referring to is, of course, forgiveness. A few years ago, we conducted a study on the effectiveness of a workshop designed to help divorced parents forgive their ex-spouse. To recruit participants, we ran ads in local newspapers and on radio stations. One day a woman named Shauna sent us an email that questioned the very point of forgiveness.

The Case of Shauna

Shauna was against the idea of forgiving her ex and wondered why anybody would sign up for our workshop. She stated that her ex didn't deserve forgiveness, because he had treated her horribly. She communicated with him through an attorney and was glad she would never have to hear his voice or see his face again. However, she found herself getting upset whenever her kids mentioned him. She said she would be open to therapy if it could "desensitize" her to hearing his name, but she also made it clear that she would be willing to consider forgiveness only after hell froze over.

Clearly, forgiving her ex was not at the top of Shauna's to-do list—the mere mention of the ex's name provoked feelings of outrage, and she viewed forgiveness as an impossible task. You don't have to be a rocket scientist (or an experienced therapist) to realize that Shauna was suffering.

Her email left us with many unanswered questions. If the idea of forgiving her ex was so outrageous, why had Shauna taken the time to write to us? Was she simply curious about why some people choose to forgive? Did she have a nagging sense that her current approach to coping with her divorce wasn't working? Was she worried that her anger toward her ex might have a negative impact on her children?

In our reply, we didn't attempt to persuade her that forgiveness would be a good idea. The decision to forgive is a deeply personal one and should be undertaken freely, without pressure. And when there's a lot of inner resistance to forgiving, it probably makes sense to hold off and focus instead on other coping strategies. Forgiveness requires a commitment to a different way of thinking, so it's best to wait until you're ready. We thanked Shauna for her letter, expressed sympathy for her suffering, and explained that some people choose to forgive because it helps them to heal following a divorce. She didn't sign up for our workshop, and we never heard from her again.

At one time or another, many divorced folks have felt that their ex doesn't deserve to be forgiven. Perhaps you have felt this way too. After all, the [insert your favorite expletive] treated you poorly, never apologized, never acknowledged that he or she hurt you, continues to act like an [insert your second favorite expletive], and doesn't seem to care how much you're suffering. On top of all that, he or she is moving on in another relationship with a total [insert your third favorite expletive] and has left you to pick up the pieces. Why would a person like that deserve your forgiveness?

These thoughts are understandable if you've been wronged deeply. However, they reveal underlying assumptions about the nature of forgiveness that deserve closer examination. Shauna assumed that forgiveness primarily benefits the offender and that it should be offered only after it has been earned. Are these assumptions correct? Can forgiveness benefit the person who forgives? Is forgiveness a reasonable response after all of the pain you have experienced? Can forgiveness help you deal with your divorce? What exactly is forgiveness anyway? We'll tackle each of these questions in this chapter.

> ## Chapter Focus
>
> This chapter explores the benefits of forgiveness after divorce. We begin with a definition of forgiveness and then present research findings on how forgiveness relates to adjustment after divorce. Finally, we encourage you to reflect upon your own readiness and willingness to forgive.

UNDERSTANDING FORGIVENESS

Before deciding whether or not you want to undertake the forgiveness journey, it's important to have a good understanding of what forgiveness is and what it's not. What are your associations with the word *forgiveness*?

EXERCISE 4.1: Your Associations with Forgiveness

GOAL   The goal of this exercise is to reflect upon your associations with forgiveness.

INSTRUCTIONS   Write down words or phrases that come to mind when you think about forgiveness. Don't think too long about this task, and try not to censor yourself. Simply allow yourself to freely associate.

After completing your list, review each association and add a plus sign next to positive associations, a minus sign next to negative associations, and an *n* next to neutral associations.

Word or Phrase	+, -, or n	Word or Phrase	+, -, or n

REFLECTION   Take a moment and look back over your list. Count up the number of positive, negative, and neutral associations with forgiveness.

Number of positive associations: _____

Number of negative associations: _____

Number of neutral associations: _____

Were most of your associations positive? Negative? Neutral? Where did you learn these associations with forgiveness?

_____

_____

If your associations were negative or neutral, are you open to considering a more positive way of thinking about forgiveness?

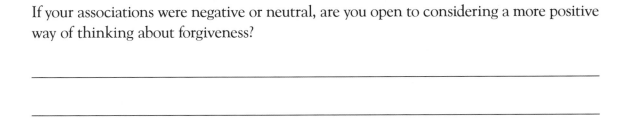

We've done this exercise with a variety of audiences, and it's always interesting to hear what people have to say. During one of our presentations, a man in his fifties who was sitting at the back of the room reported that his association with forgiveness was "No way in hell!" He declined to elaborate, but his comment cracked everyone up. Perhaps we've all felt like him at one time or another. C. S. Lewis (1952) captured this sentiment when he wrote, "Everyone says forgiveness is a lovely idea, until they have something to forgive…" (115).

Forgiveness has its share of critics. When Mark was a psychology intern at a university counseling center, each clinician was asked to offer a psychotherapy group focused on a theme or type of problem. Mark suggested a forgiveness group for people who were divorced. Little did he suspect that this idea would cause such a kerfuffle. Some clinicians were supportive and agreed that a forgiveness group would provide an interesting treatment alternative for clients. Others had serious reservations and asked some tough questions. Would a forgiveness group be appropriate for people who had experienced abuse or trauma? Could forgiveness put them at risk for being harmed again?

These were excellent questions that deserved a thoughtful response. Mark made it clear that interested individuals would be carefully screened to ensure that the group was appropriate for them. He also clarified what he meant by forgiveness. Forgiveness researchers like Enright and Fitzgibbons (2000) and McCullough, Pargament and Thoresen (2000) have argued that in order to understand what forgiveness is, you must also understand what it's not. So we'll start there.

FORGIVENESS: WHAT IT'S NOT

Forgetting. Disregard the commonly used phrase "forgive and forget." If you could forget what happened, there would be no need to forgive! One of the reasons forgiveness is so challenging is because most people remember traumatic and hurtful events. Lewis Smedes (1996), the late theologian and author, wrote, "Forgiving does not erase the bitter past. A healed memory is not a deleted memory. Instead, forgiving what we cannot forget creates a new way to remember. We change the memory of our past into a hope for our future" (171). Forgiveness can transform your memories in a way that allows you to move beyond your suffering.

Condoning or excusing. Some critics argue that forgiveness is akin to condoning or excusing the offender's behavior. This is worth addressing because sometimes people rationalize their ex's behavior and make excuses for what happened. Some even convince themselves that they deserved to be mistreated or that they brought the wrongful actions on themselves. These thoughts are problematic because they aren't true and because they put you at risk for being harmed again. However, they have nothing to do with forgiveness. Forgiveness starts with the premises that one, you don't deserve to be mistreated, and two, you won't tolerate mistreatment.

Reconciliation. Forgiveness is not the same as reconciliation. The decision to forgive depends on your readiness to let go of hurtful thoughts and feelings, whereas the decision to reconcile should take into account the offender's behavior. In some situations, reconciling with a person who has hurt you is dangerous or simply unwise. Although sometimes people hold out the hope that they can reestablish a romantic relationship with their ex, this outcome is usually not possible or desirable. More commonly, divorced folks who want to reconcile are hoping to maintain open communication, a functional co-parenting relationship, or even a friendship with their ex.

Legal pardon. If your ex committed a crime against you, forgiveness doesn't eliminate the need for your ex to face consequences through the legal system. Similarly, forgiveness doesn't mean that you have to forgo a fair divorce settlement. After all, you're faced with the considerable challenge of building a new life for yourself following the divorce, and it's only fair that you get your share of the financial resources.

Quick and easy. Forgiveness is rarely quick and easy. Granted, some people report that they forgave an offender immediately after a transgression. Others say that their long-standing feelings of anger dissipated after experiencing a sudden and dramatic change of heart. However, instantaneous forgiveness and forgiveness by epiphany are the exceptions rather than the rule. For most of us, forgiveness is a challenging process that requires time, commitment, and effort.

A sign of weakness. Mahatma Gandhi once said, "The weak can never forgive. Forgiveness is an attribute of the strong." We're not ones to disagree with Gandhi. It takes tremendous strength to forgive, particularly if you've been deeply wounded.

FORGIVENESS: WHAT IT IS

Now that we've emphasized what forgiveness is not—what the heck is it? Forgiveness involves letting go of negative feelings, thoughts, and actions toward a person who has wronged you and replacing them with a more positive approach.

Psychologist Everett Worthington et al. (2007) make a distinction between decisional and emotional forgiveness. *Decisional forgiveness* occurs when you decide to pursue forgiveness as a goal. However, just because you made this decision doesn't mean that your emotions will automatically follow suit. When you've been deeply hurt, negative feelings such as anger can easily be triggered (see chapter 1). *Emotional forgiveness*, on the other hand, involves deep transformation in which negative feelings toward an offender are replaced by more positive emotions. Emotional forgiveness often takes time and a lot of hard work. Although they may occur at different times, both decisional and emotional forgiveness are important to the forgiveness process.

WHY BOTHER WITH FORGIVENESS?

People choose to forgive for a lot of different reasons. Some forgive because they get tired of the emotional baggage they are carrying around. Others forgive out of deep religious or moral convictions. Some view forgiveness as a way to improve health and peace of mind. Parents sometimes forgive to set a good example for their kids. Regardless of your reasons, a growing body of scientific research has confirmed that forgiveness relates to positive outcomes. Here are some of them.

Forgiveness and Physical Health

Just as studies have linked hostility to poor health outcomes (see chapter 1), they have shown that forgiveness relates to better physical health. For instance, Lawler et al.

(2003) found that forgiveness related to lower blood pressure, lower heart rate, and fewer self-reported illnesses. When prompted to recall a time when a parent or caregiver hurt or upset them, forgiving participants demonstrated fewer indicators of cardiovascular distress. Another study by Lawler et al. (2005) showed that forgiveness related to fewer physical ailments, fewer medications used in the last month, less fatigue, and better sleep quality. In yet another study, when participants were instructed to focus on forgiving thoughts, they showed less physiological distress than when they were instructed to nurse grudges (Witvliet, Ludwig, and Vander Laan 2001).

Forgiveness and Mental Health

Feelings of sadness and depression are common following divorce, but studies have shown that forgiveness of an ex-spouse predicts better mood. Even after accounting for the length of time since divorce, forgiveness of an ex related to less depression (Rye et al. 2004). In addition, divorced folks who completed an eight-week secular group forgiveness intervention showed greater decreases in depression than those who did not receive the intervention (Rye et al. 2005).

Forgiveness and Parenting

Some people forgive because they want to help their children adjust to divorce. Kathryn Bonach (2005) examined how postdivorce co-parenting related to variables such as forgiveness, number of children, satisfaction with custody arrangements, length of time since the separation or divorce, satisfaction with child-support financial arrangements, and perceived severity of wrongdoing. Of all these variables, forgiveness was the best predictor of quality co-parenting relationships.

In addition to the possibility of better co-parenting, forgiveness provides children with a model for how to handle conflict. Whether or not they would admit it, kids pay attention to and learn from their parents' actions. Undertaking the forgiveness journey provides kids with an alternative model to the endless cycle of anger, recrimination, and blame that is all too common in high-conflict divorces. Think about it: what are the best lessons for children to learn about handling interpersonal conflict?

Forgiveness and Spiritual or Religious Well-Being

Many people draw upon their religious faith when trying to forgive. You don't have to be a religious or spiritual person to value forgiveness or to benefit from it. However, forgiveness is valued by the major world religions, and many religious individuals practice forgiveness. For many, forgiveness provides a means of enhancing spiritual growth. In fact, research has shown that forgiveness of an ex-spouse relates to a greater sense of religious well-being (Rye et al. 2004).

TWO POSSIBLE ROADS

The poet Robert Frost once wrote eloquently about encountering two roads that diverged in the woods. After divorce, you may encounter two diverging roads, and the road you choose matters. One road is called the Hostility Highway, and the other road is called the Forgiveness Freeway. Perhaps you are thinking, *Aren't there any other roads? I don't like either of those options!* If you find another road that helps you heal, go for it! In this book, we'll focus on these two in particular because many people hold on to feelings of bitterness following a divorce even though it prolongs their suffering. Table 3 reviews what scientific studies have discovered about hostility and forgiveness.

TABLE 3: Comparing the Hostility Highway with the Forgiveness Freeway

	Road to Hostility	**Road to Forgiveness**
Your Health	Hostility relates to chronic health problems, such as coronary heart disease and high blood pressure.	Forgiveness is associated with decreased physiological distress.
Your Mood	Hostility is related to increased depression.	Forgiveness is associated with decreased depression.
Your Adjustment to Divorce	Hostility has been linked to use of poor coping strategies.	Forgiveness of an ex-spouse relates to better postdivorce adjustment.

Parenting and Your Children's Adjustment	Hostility fuels high-conflict co-parenting. Children often feel like they are stuck in the middle when their parents argue.	Forgiveness relates to improved co-parenting and less parental conflict. Modeling forgiveness for your children may help them consider it as a strategy when they experience interpersonal conflict in their own lives.
Spiritual Well-Being	Feelings of hostility might contribute to feelings of being disconnected with God or others.	Forgiveness relates to higher levels of spiritual well-being and is consistent with the teachings of the major world religions.

If you find yourself heading down the Hostility Highway and reacting with road rage each time your ex or someone else with poor driving skills gets in your way, ask yourself some important questions: Is this road working for you? Are you finding the sense of peace that you desire? Does maintaining a grudge punish the other person or you? What consequences have you experienced (or might you experience in the future) from staying so angry?

It can be tempting to blame your ex for the fact that you are angry. While your ex is responsible for his or her hurtful actions, only you can decide which road to take in response. Even if your ex is headed at high speed down the Hostility Highway, you don't have to follow.

If you choose the Forgiveness Freeway, don't be surprised if you find yourself veering off unexpectedly in the other direction. Don't be too hard on yourself. Learning how to stay on the Forgiveness Freeway takes time and practice. Don't forget that at any point, if you want to change your direction, you can switch lanes and get off at the next exit to resume your journey down the Forgiveness Freeway. Which brings us to an important question—are you ready to work on forgiveness?

Not everyone is ready to grapple with the topic of forgiveness, and that's okay. If you've been through a lot of painful experiences, you might need to take more time to process your feelings. This is particularly true for folks who've been in abusive relationships.

Leaving an Abusive Relationship

If you have a tendency to remain in abusive relationships, we strongly advise that you hold off working on forgiveness for now, and skip over exercise 4.2 and chapter 5. Instead, we encourage you to work collaboratively with a therapist to develop a plan to keep yourself (and your children, if you're a parent) safe. As already mentioned, forgiveness has nothing to do with letting others harm you in the future. However, holding on to anger may help some people leave an abusive partner. At some point down the road, after you're safe and no longer in an abusive relationship, you'll be in a better position to work toward forgiveness if you'd like.

The next exercise invites you to reflect on your readiness to forgive by considering where you fit on the transtheoretical model of change developed by James Prochaska and Carlo DiClemente (1984). This model uses the terms *precontemplation*, *contemplation*, *preparation*, *action*, and *maintenance* to characterize readiness for change among people struggling with a variety of problems. Here these terms apply to stages of readiness to forgive.

EXERCISE 4.2: Assessing Your Desire and Readiness to Forgive

GOAL   The goal of this exercise is to reflect on your readiness to forgive and on where you are at in the forgiveness process.

INSTRUCTIONS   Consider the following descriptions of five stages of readiness to forgive and choose the one that best describes you. There are no right or wrong answers, but be honest about how you feel right now. For each stage, we provide suggestions for what to do next.

KEEP IN MIND   Remember, we strongly advise that you hold off working on forgiveness for now if you're trying to get out of an abusive relationship.

Place an X next to the stage that best describes you:

Stage	Stage Name	Description
1	Precontemplation	I'm not considering forgiving my ex and have no plans to change my mind in the near future. I object to the notion of forgiving someone who hurt me so profoundly. Forgiveness is an unrealistic goal given what I've been through. Frankly, I'm annoyed that you even brought the topic up. *Suggestion: If this is how you feel, you might want to skip chapter 5 and move ahead to chapter 6.*
2	Contemplation	I'm thinking of forgiving my ex but have not yet made a decision. *Suggestion: It's not unusual to experience some ambivalence about forgiveness. You might skip chapter 5 for now and come back to it later if you decide that you want to work toward forgiveness.*
3	Preparation	I'm getting ready to start my forgiveness journey. However, I sometimes wonder whether I can forgive my ex after everything that's happened. *Suggestion: It's okay to have doubts. Who hasn't experienced doubts about their ability to achieve a difficult goal? However, don't let doubts dissuade you from attempting the journey. If you think forgiveness might benefit you, and if you're determined to give it a try, you'll get there! We encourage you to proceed to chapter 5 for suggestions on traveling down the forgiveness path.*
4	Action	I'm fired up and ready to go. I've decided that I'm tired of the emotional baggage that I've been carrying, and I believe that forgiveness is the right path for me. I've started down the forgiveness path but still have a long way to go. *Suggestion: Read chapter 5 for ideas that will support you on your forgiveness journey.*

5	Maintenance	I've been working on forgiveness for a while now. Some days are harder than others, and sometimes an event or action triggers renewed feelings of anger or sadness. However, I'm making clear progress and want to move forward on the path.
		Suggestion: Chapter 5 provides helpful ideas for how to deal with setbacks on the forgiveness journey.

REFLECTION   Remember, whatever stage you find yourself in right now is okay. The bottom line is that you may not be ready to let go of things. Getting angry or frustrated with yourself for not being ready to let go just adds to your suffering. And don't let anybody shame you into thinking there's something wrong with you for holding on to your feelings. Keep in mind that your readiness to forgive may change over time, so it's important to periodically revisit this exercise.

WHAT'S NEXT?

If you're ready to begin working on letting go of your negative feelings toward your ex and others who have hurt you in the divorce process, or you want to continue on the forgiveness journey that you've already started, the next chapter provides helpful tips for making progress. If you're not ready to work on forgiving those who've hurt you, skip ahead to chapter 6.

CHAPTER 5

"I Can't Seem to Let My Feelings Go"

Learning How to Forgive

Deciding to forgive is one thing. Getting there can be quite another. There's no question that forgiving your ex or anyone else who has hurt you during the divorce can be a challenging task. One of the reasons it can be so difficult is that forgiveness brings us into unfamiliar territory. Anger, resentment, and sadness may be painful, but they are often familiar feelings.

Forgiveness requires a new and courageous way of thinking about those who wronged you. When forgiving, you must draw upon your deepest inner resources as you seek to transform painful experiences into something that will help you to grow as a person.

Chapter Focus

This chapter offers some helpful strategies for preparing and working toward forgiveness following divorce. We also discuss some obstacles that you may face when trying to forgive.

PREPARING TO FORGIVE

A few things can make your journey smoother as you prepare to work toward forgiveness. Even if you've been on the forgiveness journey for some time, you may find it helpful to review these ideas.

Take One Step at a Time

The thought of forgiving your ex or someone else who hurt you deeply during the divorce can seem overwhelming. It's kind of like climbing a tall mountain. Nobody can climb a mountain in a single step; instead you need to take many steps to reach the summit. If you focus on how steep the mountain is, how hard you are working, how many steps you still have to take, or the possibility that there's a grizzly bear over the next hill, you'll become disheartened. On the other hand, if you focus on your next step forward, and nothing more, the task seems much less daunting. By the way, as you climb toward forgiveness, make sure you take some time to savor the view.

Be Compassionate Toward Yourself

Try not to judge yourself as you undertake the forgiveness process. You're likely to encounter setbacks and challenges along the way, and that's okay. Berating yourself for struggling with forgiveness will only make your journey harder. You might find it helpful to review some of the self-compassion exercises in chapter 3 as you get started.

Be Open to New Ways of Thinking

When your car is stuck in the mud, stepping on the gas harder can make things worse. Similarly, clinging tenaciously to the assumptions that got you mired in feelings of anger and bitterness is not a good strategy for moving forward. However, if you're willing to turn the wheel a bit, and entertain the possibility that there are other ways of thinking about your ex and others who've hurt you, you can move forward again.

FORGIVENESS STRATEGIES

No single approach to forgiveness works for everyone, because each of us brings a unique set of experiences, perspectives, and genetic predispositions to the process. The secret is to adopt forgiveness strategies that will work for you. Fortunately, you can draw upon research findings, established forgiveness programs, and the experiences of people who've already traveled down this road for tips on how to get to your destination. Here are eight strategies that can help you forgive. Although the focus here is on forgiving your ex, these strategies can easily be applied to forgiving anyone else who has hurt you deeply.

Strategy 1: Let Go of the Small Stuff

On your first day of training for a marathon, it's probably best not to start with a 26.2-mile run. If you haven't been physically active for a while, you might begin with an easier aerobic activity, like walking around the block a few times. Similarly when forgiving, why not start by letting go of the easy stuff?

Take a moment and revisit your grudge inventory in exercise 1.1, where you identified the grudge that would be easiest to let go. Start by trying to let that grudge go. When working to let go of this grudge, you might start by noticing whenever your thoughts turn to the transgression. As noted in chapter 2, becoming more aware of your thoughts and then allowing them to dissipate can diminish the power that the thoughts have over you. Make a commitment to shift your focus from the transgression to the benefits that await once you let go of your grudge. You could imagine yourself leaving behind a heavy object that represents the transgression so that you'll be carrying less weight moving forward. Other suggestions for how to let go of grudges are provided later in this chapter, so keep reading.

Every time you let go of a grudge, you'll feel a little lighter and will gain confidence that you can tackle the tougher hurts down the road. As you exercise your forgiveness muscles, they'll become stronger.

Strategy 2: Express Your Intention to Forgive

When your goals are clearly defined, it's easier to take steps in the right direction. Why not start by declaring that forgiveness is your desired destination? This can be as simple as making a promise to yourself. Or you could tell a trusted friend, your therapist, or a religious leader about your plan. However, telling your ex could make things worse, especially if your ex never acknowledged hurting you in the first place. We advise against telling your ex unless he or she is genuinely remorseful and is asking for your forgiveness.

We invite you to write a letter addressed to your ex-spouse—but don't send the letter! This letter is for you, not your ex.

EXERCISE 5.1: The Unmailed Letter

GOAL   The goal of this exercise is to express in writing your commitment to pursue forgiveness.

INSTRUCTIONS   Write a letter to your ex describing why you decided to work toward forgiving him or her. This letter can be as long or as short as you would like. You can write the letter in one sitting or over the course of several days. (After completing this exercise, some people discover that they've written a short novel.) If you need room beyond the space provided, you can use your journal to continue writing.

If people other than your ex have hurt you deeply, consider writing a separate letter to each of them.

VARIATIONS   If you don't like writing letters or aren't good at expressing yourself in writing, consider one of the following variations.

Option 1: An audio message. Record an audio message that explains why you decided to work toward forgiveness. You could talk into a tablet computer, smartphone, or (gasp!) even a tape recorder.

Option 2: Artistic reflection. If you're artistically inclined, you could reflect on your decision to forgive through creating music, poetry, short stories, or a painting.

KEEP IN MIND   Remember, the purpose of this exercise is to reflect upon your feelings and express your desire to forgive—not to cause conflict. So please don't mail this letter or share it with your ex! Also, remember to keep this letter in a safe place, so it won't be discovered by someone who isn't supposed to read it.

Date: _____

Dear _____,

_____

_____

_____

_____

_____

_____

_____

_____

_____

_____

REFLECTION   Briefly describe how it felt to express your intention to forgive.

_____

_____

_____

What insights did you gain from your letter, audio recording, or artistic creation?

_____

_____

_____

_____

You might want to spend some time discussing your letter with a close friend, your divorce support group, or a therapist.

Strategy 3: Focus on an Inspirational Role Model

Is there someone in your life who can serve as an inspirational role model for forgiveness? A member of your divorce support group? A friend? A parent? A grandparent? A sibling? Your fourth cousin twice removed?

If nobody comes to mind, consider picking a guide whom you don't know personally. If you love novels, is there a character whose decision to forgive inspired you? (Jean Valjean from _Les Misérables_ comes to Mark's mind.) If you're religious, is there someone from religious scripture who can teach you about forgiveness? You could also do an Internet search for autobiographical material on forgiveness and read firsthand accounts of people who have forgiven despite being hurt profoundly.

Strategy 4: Expand and Shift Your Focus

Watching the evening news is usually not an uplifting experience. While the content of the stories changes from day to day, the recurrent themes are generally natural disasters, violent crimes, political squabbling, and wars (with a feel-good story thrown in at the end about the rescue of a runaway red panda). The majority of the news is decidedly negative and pessimistic, and sometimes it can be hard to remember that what you're watching onscreen is not representative of everything that's happening.

Similarly, as you replay the events of the divorce in your mind, it's easy to get caught up in the drama of it all and forget that there's other programming available. This idea was presented by Fred Luskin (2002), author of *Forgive for Good*, who likens your thought processes, after you've been wronged, to watching television. Luskin points out that if you get in the habit of watching the Grievance Channel, your sense of outrage and feelings of hostility will be strengthened. On the other hand, there's other programming available, and you can change the channel whenever you want. Luskin points out that you can tune into the Beauty Channel, the Love Channel, the Gratitude Channel, and the Forgiveness Channel. In fact, all of the positive psychology strategies presented in this book are examples of what you can focus on besides feelings of anger, hurt, and resentment.

Strategy 5: Draw Upon Your Faith

People often turn to their religious faith when going through tough times or when trying to accomplish a difficult task. For instance, some people are able to forgive through prayer. Lambert et al. (2010) ran two studies examining the effect of prayer on forgiveness. In the first study, they found that participants assigned to pray for their romantic partner were more willing to forgive than participants who engaged in an alternative activity. In the second study, they found that people who were instructed to pray for a friend who'd hurt them scored higher on forgiveness than participants who prayed about another topic or who simply focused on positive thoughts toward their friend.

Not everyone who values prayer wants to pray for the person who wronged them. Even so, there are other ways that prayer might be helpful in the forgiveness process. Some folks rely on prayer as a means of drawing comfort and support whenever they are facing a difficult challenge. (Working on forgiving your ex definitely qualifies as such!) Other people prefer contemplative prayer, in which they try to quiet their minds and listen to inner or divine wisdom for how to think and act. If prayer is an important part of your life, you might want to give it a try when working on forgiveness. If prayer isn't your thing, consider focusing on mindfulness meditation (see chapter 2) for changing your perspective about your ex.

Strategy 6: Think of a Time When You Did Something Hurtful

It's easy to criticize others for their outrageous behavior; most of us find it much harder to honestly look at our own. Yet all of the major world religions urge us to reflect

101

upon our own shortcomings. For example, the holiest day of the year in the Jewish calendar, Yom Kippur, involves deep reflection and atonement for one's sins. In the Christian New Testament, Jesus asks why we focus on the speck in our neighbor's eye but not the log in our own eye. When you're having difficulty overlooking the shortcomings of others, it can be helpful to take a few moments to reflect upon your own.

Have you ever done or said something that was hurtful? The purpose of this question is to humanize your ex—not to suggest that you deserved to be hurt (because you did not) or to make you feel bad about yourself. If you're experiencing significant shame or guilt over actions you have taken in the past and are having a hard time moving forward, please check out chapter 6 for some helpful suggestions.

Strategy 7: Empathize with Your Ex

You may be thinking, *What? You want me to empathize with my ex? After everything that's happened? After what my family has gone through?* Yes—if you want to make progress with forgiveness. We recognize that trying to identify with what your ex is feeling can be really difficult at first. If you're not ready to work on this, that's okay. Skip ahead to the next forgiveness strategy. However, we urge you to come back to this when you can, because research has shown that developing empathy toward the person who hurt you is one of the secrets to being able to forgive (McCullough, Worthington, and Rachal 1997; Riek and Mania 2012).

What follows are some suggestions for increasing your empathy toward your ex. They may require you to challenge your current way of thinking. Again, if any of these suggestions are too uncomfortable given your current frame of mind, it would be better to hold off for now. However, if you're feeling ready, take these ideas out for a spin and see if they soften your views about your ex.

CONSIDER HOW YOUR EX IS SUFFERING

Think of a time you experienced intense physical pain. Perhaps you injured yourself or you have had pain due to a chronic health condition. Throbbing pain demands your immediate attention, and when you feel it, it can be hard to think about anything else. The same thing can be true with emotional pain. When you're suffering deeply, it can be hard to notice anything else. It can be particularly hard to recognize that your ex is suffering when it doesn't fit with the story you've developed about the divorce. Consider the following case.

The Case of Joanna

Joanna lives in the same small town as her ex, Alicia, and runs into her frequently. Alicia takes every opportunity she can to berate Joanna in front of friends and coworkers about Joanna's "failures" during their marriage. Joanna finds this deeply embarrassing and is angry that Alicia won't leave her alone. One day, after yet another unpleasant interaction with Alicia, Joanna noticed that Alicia didn't look well. Maybe the financial strain of the divorce had started to affect her health. Maybe she was depressed and had stopped taking care of herself. Joanna saw for the first time that underneath all of her animosity Alicia was suffering.

Joanna's heart softened somewhat from that moment on. Although Joanna still becomes angry at times, she began to view Alicia through a more compassionate lens and recognized that Alicia's personal problems were making it difficult for her to move on with her life.

The next exercise invites you to consider some of the ways that your ex has suffered following the divorce. Remember, empathizing with your ex is not the same as excusing or condoning hurtful actions. Moreover, acknowledging that your ex is suffering doesn't diminish the fact that you've suffered.

EXERCISE 5.2: Acknowledging Ways Your Ex May Be Suffering

GOAL   This exercise asks you to reflect on how your ex may be suffering, which can help you let go of your negative feelings.

INSTRUCTIONS   List three ways that your ex has suffered (or may be suffering) since the divorce.

KEEP IN MIND   This exercise can be really challenging, particularly if it appears on the surface that everything is going well for your ex and everything is going poorly for you. However, if you're willing to look deeply and with an open heart, you'll become more aware of ways that your ex is experiencing challenges.

If you're having difficulty with this exercise, choose something small. You could even list something that your ex struggled with while you were still married.

Three Ways Your Ex Has Suffered

Example 1: *My ex has had financial problems since the divorce.*

Example 2: *My ex doesn't have close friends to confide in and has been dealing with the divorce alone.*

1.

2.

3.

REFLECTION   What was it like for you to complete this task?

_____

_____

Of the things you listed, did anything surprise you?

_____

_____

How might thinking about your ex's suffering help you forgive your ex?

_____

_____

_____

RECONSIDER THE REASONS FOR YOUR EX'S BEHAVIOR

When treated like crap (this is the technical term that therapists use), most of us are motivated to explain why the other person acted the way he or she did. Psychologists call these explanations *attributions*, and they help us make sense of the world. Interestingly, the explanation that you give for someone else's behavior is likely to differ from the explanation you'd give if the behavior were your own.

Think about the last time you were cut off by another driver. Perhaps you were startled or upset because the other driver's actions could've caused an accident. What was your immediate explanation for why the driver cut you off? If you're like many people, you might have said, "What a jerk!" or "That loser doesn't know how to drive!" (We know you used stronger language, but we have to get this past our editors.)

Now, think about the last time you cut someone off while driving (admit it, we've all done this at some point). How did you explain your driving faux pas? Did you say, "I'm such a jerk and I don't know how to drive"? (If so, please warn us next time you're out on the road.) More likely you took into account extenuating circumstances: "My screaming infant in the back seat distracted me," "I was dealing with serious back pain that day," "The song on the radio was so bad that I had to change it immediately," or "The other driver was driving too slow."

The more inclined you are to focus exclusively on your ex's character flaws and ignore other possible explanations, the harder it will be to forgive. On the extreme end are folks who demonize their exes and believe that they are the cause of everything that's wrong in the world.

Perhaps your ex does have character flaws that prompt him or her to treat others poorly. If so, there's no need to deny or gloss over the fact that your ex interacts with others in fundamentally problematic ways. However, it's your decision either to focus on those flaws and demonize your ex or to search for alternative ways of thinking that will make it easier to move on from the anger and hurt that you've been carrying around.

Joanna's perspective changed when she considered the complex factors that contributed to Alicia's hurtful behavior. Alicia's parents were poor role models for how to have a healthy marriage. Alicia was recently laid off from work and is having trouble getting another job. Alicia also struggles with depression. None of these factors excuse Alicia's hurtful behavior. However, they provided some context that enabled Joanna to look at their strained interactions from a fresh perspective.

The next exercise asks you to think in new ways about possible reasons for your ex's behavior.

EXERCISE 5.3: New Perspectives on Your Ex's Behavior

GOAL The goal of this exercise is to consider alternative explanations for your ex's behavior, which can help you let go of negative feelings.

INSTRUCTIONS Pick three of your ex's behaviors that annoy or hurt you. Consider explanations for these behaviors that focus on circumstances and past experiences rather than on character flaws.

KEEP IN MIND The goal is not to excuse your ex's behavior or to make your ex any less responsible for his or her actions. Nor does this exercise imply that your initial explanations are necessarily wrong. Nevertheless, there's value in brainstorming other ways of thinking about your ex if you're stuck in feelings of anger and resentment.

Don't worry about coming up with the "correct" set of reasons for your ex's behavior. Instead, use this exercise as a reminder that the reasons why people behave the way they do are often complex and that your judgments about their actions are based on incomplete information.

Annoying or Hurtful Behavior	Your Standard Explanation (Which Isn't Necessarily Wrong)	Alternative Explanations
Example: *My ex always criticizes me.*	*My ex is mean-spirited.*	1. *My ex grew up in a home where there wasn't much love or affection.* 2. *Things aren't going very well right now in my ex's life.*
		1. 2.

		1. 2.
		1. 2.

REFLECTION   How easy or difficult was this exercise for you and why?

_____

_____

_____

If you had trouble with this exercise, be assured that you aren't the only one! Consider working on this exercise again at a later date, and pay attention to whether it becomes easier over time.

Strategy 8: Develop a Forgiveness Ritual

Artist Karen Green created a forgiveness machine after experiencing heartache in her own life (Adams 2011). The machine, which was seven feet long, appeared in a Pasadena art gallery. People could write down on a piece of paper whatever they wanted to forgive, and after the paper was placed in the machine, it was sucked in by a vacuum and then shredded. Green observed that visitors to the exhibit often became quite emotional when using the machine. It drew quite a crowd and eventually had to be disassembled due to overuse.

Wouldn't it be great if forgiveness were as simple as that? Although a machine can't take the place of the inner work that's necessary for forgiveness, it's helpful to create a ritual that symbolizes your decision to let go of hurts that have been weighing you down. Rituals mark important changes and can provide a sense of comfort and predictability when life seems to be out of control. That's why forgiveness experts often incorporate rituals into programs designed to help people forgive.

In one version of a treatment program we offered, group leaders gave divorced group members an ugly rock, which was intended to symbolize all of the pain and hardship they had experienced because of their ex's hurtful actions. The leaders explained that group members could do whatever they wanted with the rock. The variety of ways that they handled the rock over the next week was interesting. Several members held on to the rock because they weren't ready to forgive yet. One group member buried the rock in her backyard. Another painted the rock, transforming it into something beautiful. Several group members joked about wanting to throw the rock through their ex's window, but fortunately nobody did that!

EXERCISE 5.4: The Forgiveness Ritual

GOAL   The goal of this two-part exercise is to design and carry out a forgiveness ritual that symbolizes your willingness to forgive.

INSTRUCTIONS FOR PART A   Design a forgiveness ritual that would be meaningful to you. List your ideas in the space provided. You could borrow from the ideas in this book or develop your own.

KEEP IN MIND   This exercise works best after you've been working on forgiveness for a while. That way, your ritual can be a symbol of both the progress you've already made and your desire to continue down the forgiveness path.

Ideas for Forgiveness Rituals

Example 1: *Write down my grudges and burn them in the fireplace.*

Example 2: *Let go of helium balloons outside and watch them float away as a symbol of my desire to let go of my burdens.*

1.

2.

3.

4.

INSTRUCTIONS FOR PART B   Look back over your list and circle the ritual that would be most meaningful for you. Then, set aside a time when you have no other distractions, and carry out the ritual.

KEEP IN MIND   Remember, you should do this only when you're ready. If you would rather wait until more time has passed, that's okay. When you're ready, consider inviting a close friend to observe. Having a friend nearby can remind you that you don't have to go through this process alone.

REFLECTION   What was it like to engage in this activity? What feelings came up for you in the process?

_____

_____

_____

_____

_____

_____

ANTICIPATING OBSTACLES TO FORGIVENESS

Are you familiar with the television show *Wipeout?* If not, it's a reality game-show series that features contestants trying to navigate a challenging obstacle course in the fastest time possible. The obstacles are large and intimidating, and, more often than not, contestants bounce off of them in spectacular fashion and splash into the water below. Similarly, the path toward forgiveness poses some enormous challenges. Sometimes you smack right into obstacles, bounce off, and get knocked off course. But getting knocked off course on your forgiveness journey doesn't mean you can't make it to your destination. You just have to regroup and find a different way to approach the obstacle in the future.

As you undertake the forgiveness journey, being able to anticipate possible challenges along the way will help you handle them effectively when they arise.

Obstacle 1: Severity of Wrongdoing

Not surprisingly, the more deeply you've been hurt, the more difficult it can be to forgive. Like Shauna from chapter 4, some divorced folks believe that the wrongdoing committed by their ex was so egregious, so profound, and so morally reprehensible that forgiveness is impossible. If this is how you feel, we aren't going to try to talk you out of this position. Only you can decide if you want to pursue forgiveness under these circumstances. However, it is possible to forgive after serious transgressions if you decide this is the right path for you.

POSSIBLE SOLUTION

Pick a role model of someone who has forgiven someone else after being wronged in a terrible way. Perhaps you know of someone personally who fits this description. If not, you can draw inspiration from authors who forgave the perpetrators of terrible crimes. For instance, Everett Worthington Jr. (2003) has written about his decision to forgive the person who murdered his mother. Similarly, Marietta Jaeger (1998) wrote about her decision to forgive the person who kidnapped and murdered her daughter.

Although some people find it difficult to imagine forgiving perpetrators of such heinous crimes, Worthington and Jaeger believed that forgiveness was the best path forward for them. If you have experienced a terrible wrongdoing, only you can decide if forgiveness is the path for you.

Obstacle 2: Absence of Apology, Remorse, or Restitution

It's easier to forgive when the person who has hurt you apologizes, shows remorse, or tries to make things right. Studies have shown that conciliatory gestures make forgiveness easier because they make the transgressor appear more agreeable, considerate, and fair (Tabak et al. 2012). Unfortunately, many ex-spouses never apologize or acknowledge that their actions have caused suffering. If you're willing to forgive only after your ex shows contrition, you may be waiting until the cows come home!

POSSIBLE SOLUTION

Try to focus on the benefits that forgiveness has for you. If you believe that forgiveness will help you heal, why would you let your ex's failure to apologize or make amends impede your progress?

Obstacle 3: Frequent Reminders of How You Were Hurt

Folks who continue interacting with their ex, by either choice or necessity, are faced with frequent reminders of how they were hurt. Ongoing interactions with someone who hurt you can trigger classically conditioned feelings of anger (see chapter 1). Here are some examples:

- Living in a small town or near your ex

- Facing protracted legal proceedings related to the divorce or to custody arrangements

- Sharing mutual friends

- Working in the same organization or profession

- Chance encounters

- Co-parenting

- Special events for your children (school plays, graduations, weddings)

Although encountering your ex in these situations can be difficult, you can shift your focus away from the negative thoughts and feelings that emerge so that you can handle these situations from a position of emotional strength.

POSSIBLE SOLUTION

Whenever you find yourself getting stuck thinking about how you were wronged, try to focus on things that will be uplifting to you. You might even set a strict limit on how much time you'll allow yourself to focus on your grievances each day.

Obstacle 4: Your Ex Still Engages in Hurtful Behavior

It's challenging enough if you have to interact with your ex, but what if your ex continues to act in hurtful ways? One participant who attended our divorce workshop observed, "It's hard to forgive when you are in the middle of a car wreck."

POSSIBLE SOLUTION

Remember, forgiveness does not mean that you allow yourself to get walked on. "When we forgive someone who is not sorry for what he has done, we do not forget, and we do not intend to let it happen again" (Smedes 1996, 92).

If you have ongoing communication with your ex, talk to people you can trust who will give you objective advice on how to handle your ex's shenanigans. It's important to develop strategies that work for your unique situation, but here are a few guidelines:

- Although you can't control your ex's behavior, try to limit opportunities that your ex has to hurt you.

- Make it clear that you're willing to communicate with your ex only when he or she acts in a civil manner. If your ex does not act civilly, politely end the conversation and make it clear that you will continue only after he or she cools down.

- Try to filter out any nastiness or verbal attacks in your communication and focus on getting the vital information across.

- When talking with your ex, avoid starting any sentences with "You always do this" because it'll put your ex on the defensive. Instead, try "When you do X, Y, and Z, I feel…"

- When your ex is picking an argument, don't immediately launch into a lecture on why your ex's perspective is wrong. Instead, summarize his or her point of view as best as you can and check to see if you got it right. You'll be amazed as how this strategy can turn the temperature down on a heated conversation.

- Seek assistance from the court if your ex is violating terms of the divorce or your custody agreement.

Hopefully, using these strategies will improve your communication with your ex. Knowing that you're doing the best that you can in dealing with your ex may also help you with forgiveness.

Obstacle 5: Something Sacred Was Violated

Forgiveness can be especially difficult when your ex has violated something that you consider sacred. For example, many folks view marriage as a sacred relationship. When marital vows are violated, it can be especially painful because your most deeply cherished values have been affected.

POSSIBLE SOLUTION

If you're religious, it can be helpful to read scriptures or talk to religious leaders about alternative ways of thinking about what happened. In many religious traditions, forgiveness is a sacred act that can enhance a sense of connection with God and others.

Obstacle 6: People Around You Haven't Forgiven

It's hard to stay on the Forgiveness Freeway when everyone around you is traveling down the Hostility Highway. Are there people around you who are reinforcing your angry feelings? If so, this isn't surprising. People who care about you might hold their own grudges against your ex because of the suffering you've endured, and they might think they are supporting you by saying unkind things about your ex. Working toward forgiveness can also be difficult if your divorced friends are constantly talking about how much they hate their exes.

POSSIBLE SOLUTION

Although complaining about your ex is understandable, at some point it can interfere with your desire to let go and move on. If you're around family or divorced friends when they're complaining about your ex (or theirs), you don't have to join in. You could try gently changing the subject or explaining that you're trying to move on, because focusing on your ex's hurtful actions makes you feel bad. If friends and family are sensitive to your needs, they'll get the picture. Also, try to surround yourself with a few people who will support you in your journey toward forgiveness. If this support can't be found in your existing social network, you may need to branch out and make some new friends.

YOUR FORGIVENESS JOURNEY

This chapter has covered just a few of the obstacles that divorced folks face when trying to forgive. Perhaps you are facing obstacles of a different sort. We invite you to take a moment to reflect upon the obstacles you face on your forgiveness journey along with possible ways to overcome them.

EXERCISE 5.5: Your Forgiveness Obstacles

GOAL   The objective is to reflect upon your personal obstacles on the forgiveness journey and possible ways to overcome them.

INSTRUCTIONS   Take a moment to think about the obstacles that make forgiving your ex (or anyone else related to your divorce) especially challenging. List them in the obstacles column. Then try to come up with two strategies for overcoming each obstacle.

Obstacles	Plans for Overcoming Obstacles
Example: *Every time I run into my ex, I think about everything she did to me.*	1. *Remind myself that holding on to a grudge is hurting me more than my ex.* 2. *Read an inspirational story about a person who forgave despite being hurt deeply.*
	1. 2.
	1. 2.
	1. 2.
	1. 2.

REFLECTION   Count the number of forgiveness obstacles that you listed. Are you facing a lot of obstacles in your forgiveness path? Do you ever find this discouraging?

_____

_____

_____

_____

If you're discouraged, think about a time in your life when you achieved an important goal despite difficult obstacles. Remember, the presence of obstacles doesn't mean that you can't attain your goal. It just means that you'll have to be thoughtful about how to handle obstacles when they arise.

Did you have trouble coming up with ideas for getting around these obstacles? Often, obstacles to forgiveness can be overcome by simply taking a different perspective, but sometimes you need to take action. Ask someone who is trustworthy and who understands your circumstances to help you brainstorm ways to work around the obstacles that you are facing.

Everyone faces obstacles on their forgiveness journey. You may find that new and unexpected ones crop up from time to time. Try not to let these challenges discourage you or deter you from your path. Instead, use them as an opportunity to increase your determination to leave your painful emotions in the past so that your present and future can be full of new and exciting possibilities. Remember that forgiveness is a process that usually takes time. Regardless of whether your forgiveness journey lasts a few months or many years, the important thing is to keep moving in the right direction. Please be kind and loving toward yourself as you encounter the ups and downs of working toward forgiveness. Take a moment from time to time to appreciate the fact that in spite of everything you have been through, you've chosen to pursue the courageous path of forgiveness. Remind yourself of the positive ways in which your decision to forgive can help you and the people you love.

WHAT'S NEXT?

We encourage you to return to this chapter periodically as you make progress down the path of forgiving your ex and anyone else who has hurt you. Keep in mind that there's another person you may want to forgive after you've gone through a divorce—yourself. Chapter 6 will tackle the topic of self-forgiveness.

CHAPTER 6

"How Did I Screw Up So Badly?"

Letting Go of Guilt and Shame

Mistakes are an inevitable part of being human, and in the context of divorce, they can seem magnified. As imperfect human beings, we've all messed up, and it's inevitable that we'll screw up in the future! Making mistakes isn't the real problem—it's how you think about them and what you do next that's critical.

There are a lot of different ways to handle misdeeds. For example, you may become crippled by shame or—at the other end of the spectrum—blame others for your blunders. Alternatively, you can try to see how you contribute to the messes in your life, and take the appropriate amount of responsibility for that role. How you internally manage your own errors shapes how you respond behaviorally. Do you tend to make the same mistakes over and over? Are you feeling stuck? Can you use your slipups as a foundation for growth and change? Are you able to be compassionate and forgiving toward yourself?

We'd like to introduce you to Cara, who, as all of us have from time to time, has made a mess of things.

The Case of Cara

Cara just received notice that her divorce is final. Her best friend suggested that they go out for dinner to celebrate, but Cara doesn't feel very festive. Although she believes that a divorce was best for her and her ex-husband Gary, she can't shake her guilt and shame about the things she did to contribute to the breakup of her marriage. Early on, when Cara first became aware of the cracks starting to form in their relationship, she repeatedly asked Gary to go to counseling with her. He refused, telling her that she was the one who needed the help, not him. He also said that he was too busy at work and couldn't take the time off. Cara had never been to counseling and was afraid. She couldn't muster the courage to go alone although she knew deep down that she needed professional assistance to help address her intensifying drinking problem and her crumbling relationship.

Although she's been sober for about six months now, the end of Cara's marriage is a hazy recollection of events colored by alcohol abuse. Since the age of sixteen, Cara had been a binge drinker, and her drinking became unmanageable over the past two years, which coincided with her marriage falling apart. While Cara drank, Gary found his drug of choice in work. He put in about seventy hours a week at the office, which helped him climb the corporate ladder. While Gary's attention was focused elsewhere, Cara invested her time in a series of alcohol-fueled liaisons with men she met online and in bars. Cara, who is normally shy and inhibited, found that she could be a different person when she was drinking—funny, outgoing, sexy. She found that her good friend Booze gave her the courage to connect with people.

At the time, Cara rationalized that Gary didn't care what she did, and her lies came fast and easy. This all came crashing down when she was arrested for drunk driving one night when returning from one of her "dates." Gary was out of town on business at the time, so Cara had to call her father to bail her out. Although Cara had never been in trouble with the law before, she lost her job as a visiting nurse when her driver's license was suspended.

Cara let a lot of people down (including herself) and put the safety of others at risk, and the shame and guilt she feels is tearing her up. Although she is beginning to heal her relationship with her parents, Cara can't get past the shame she feels over all of the damage she has caused. She can't believe she is "that type of person."

Depending on your perspective, Cara's situation may or may not be extreme, but all of us have committed acts for which we need to forgive ourselves. Interestingly, in our work with clients who are going through a divorce, people often remark that they can forgive others more easily than they can forgive themselves. As noted in chapter 3, many folks have a tendency to be hard on themselves, and this can come from society's messages as well as what your parents and other family members modeled for you growing up. Like Cara you may be having a hard time coping with shame or feelings of guilt surrounding your divorce. But, like Cara, not forgiving yourself can keep you stuck facing the same negative emotions time and time again.

Chapter Focus

This chapter takes a look at what self-forgiveness is and how it might benefit you as you navigate the divorce process. If you're convinced that you want to let go of shame, guilt, and other negative emotions, we will guide you through some steps you can take to work toward forgiving yourself.

WHAT IS SELF-FORGIVENESS?

Self-forgiveness is different from letting yourself off the hook for mistakes. Self-forgiveness can be defined as "a willingness to abandon self-resentment in the face of one's own acknowledged objective wrong, while fostering compassion, generosity, and love toward oneself" (Enright 1996, 115). Philosopher Margaret Holmgren (1998) argued that self-forgiveness involves three broad elements: an objective wrongdoing, overcoming negative emotions associated with the wrongdoing, and eventual self-acceptance.

It makes sense that you first have to notice you've done something wrong before you can forgive yourself for it, right? Sometimes you may not realize you've hurt someone until it's pointed out to you. At the other extreme, you may have a raging self-critic inside that is quick to come up with scenarios in which you may have hurt others. That's why the definitions by Enright and Holmgren include the word "objective" to describe the wrongdoing. The process of self-forgiveness involves clearly seeing what you've done to hurt others.

Another part of the process is squarely dealing with the negative emotions that arise as a result of your hurtful actions. Suffering occurs when you actively resist your pain. There's no doubt it hurts like hell to face the fact that you may have lied to your ex about finances, been unfaithful, put the kids in the middle of arguments, been emotionally unavailable—whatever your transgressions may have been. But, as you've come to realize, running or hiding from that guilt, self-loathing, or fear really doesn't work in the long run. There's no going around these emotions—you've got to go through them.

Take Cara's case. Cara is bogged down in a morass of shame and guilt and, as a result, she's having a difficult time finding the energy to actively look for a job in her field. Although she's working in a temporary service position, she's a gifted and compassionate nurse. But for Cara to look for a job in health care, she would likely have to explain to prospective employers why she lost her previous position and how she's working hard in her recovery. Even if she does that, her efforts may not be fruitful; she might not find an organization willing to hire her at this point. She's not willing to take the risk to move forward.

Moving forward can be hard—it's risky, and full of unknowns. Sometimes staying where you are may be easier. Do you feel stuck emotionally? As painful as it can be, you may be stuck because you're getting something out of it!

When we've suggested to clients that being stuck might work for them on some level, they're often incredulous ("You think I like being this miserable? You're saying I'm choosing this?"). We aren't saying that people revel in their misery, but there are reasons why people choose not to move forward. How about you? How willing are you to move through your difficult emotions to reconcile with and accept yourself and your current situation? What function does being stuck serve? The next exercise explores this.

EXERCISE 6.1: Cultivating a Willingness to Move Forward

GOAL   The goal of this exercise is to help you cultivate an authentic willingness to move forward emotionally as you deal with your divorce.

INSTRUCTIONS   Take a moment to assess the degree to which, as a result of your divorce, you're feeling stuck in your ability to move forward emotionally. To help you process this question, you may want to write in your journal, talk to a trusted confidant, or just take some time to reflect. Answer the questions that follow based on your assessment.

KEEP IN MIND   This exercise isn't easy. In fact, we don't expect that you'll breeze through any of the exercises in this chapter. Complete this exercise with as much self-compassion as possible. Be kind to yourself as you do this work!

QUESTIONS   Rate yourself on how stuck you feel on a scale from 1 to 10, where 1 means you're able to easily move through the difficult emotions related to your divorce and 10 means you're completely unable to let go and move forward: _____

Write down the emotions you're experiencing that may be keeping you stuck. For example, fear keeps some people from moving forward, or anger might prevent growth.

_____

_____

Are there any benefits to being stuck emotionally? This may be hard to answer at first, but take a few moments to see if you can come up with something. (It may help to recall how Cara was benefiting from being stuck.)

_____

_____

_____

_____

_____

What do you stand to gain if you move toward becoming unstuck and healing emotionally?

_____

_____

_____

_____

_____

_____

Based on this analysis, how willing are you to move forward? Are you ready to give up whatever staying stuck is providing?

_____

_____

_____

_____

Being willing to move toward self-forgiveness and acceptance is half the battle. Without that willingness, there's no true engagement with the work necessary to push forward.

Pseudo vs. Authentic Self-Forgiveness

At times people may claim they have forgiven themselves when, in reality, they never took responsibility for their actions in the first place. Instead, they rationalize their behavior and make excuses. This is not authentic self-forgiveness but what psychologists call *pseudo self-forgiveness*.

Authentic self-forgiveness involves a sustained effort in working through your feelings, experiencing remorse, and accepting responsibility for your role in the wrongdoing (Fisher and Exline 2010; Hall and Fincham 2005). It's one thing to acknowledge that you've messed up but quite another to take responsibility for it. Without truly owning up to your role in causing the hurt, you might rationalize the behavior or make excuses (Holmgren 2002), which may lead to the same problematic behaviors in the future. Sitting and being with your feelings of guilt, regret, and other painful emotions prompted by the transgression is also part of the authentic self-forgiveness process. All of this takes time and effort. Given the possible benefits, we think it's worth it. But you can be the judge.

Possible Benefits of Self-Forgiveness

Research suggests that those who forgive themselves have lower levels of anxiety, depression, and shame and higher levels of well-being and life satisfaction (Macaskill 2012; Maltby, Macaskill and Day 2001; Mauger et al. 1992; Ross et al. 2004; Thompson et al. 2005). Scherer et al. (2011) found that participants assigned to a four-hour self-forgiveness intervention had decreased feelings of guilt and shame about their transgressions compared to those who completed another treatment.

Among the first researchers to look at self-forgiveness through a scientific lens were psychologist Paul Mauger and colleagues, who theorized that people who were unforgiving toward themselves had an *intropunitive* style (Mauger et al. 1992). People with this style see themselves as shameful, damaged, and unworthy of acceptance, and they are quick to internalize blame. So it's pretty easy to see that with this mind-set you'd be more likely to experience worry and depression. This is just another way of thinking about that raging inner critic we've talked about before. On the flip side, those who are compassionate and gentle with themselves tend to be more satisfied with life and less depressed and anxious.

Are you ready to work toward self-forgiveness? If so, we invite you to fully engage with the upcoming exercises in this chapter. This work isn't easy or comfortable, but the rewards can be great. As noted by Pubilius Syrus, a slave living in Rome in the first century, "The sweetest pleasure arises from difficulties overcome." And when working on self-forgiveness, one common difficulty is dealing with shame.

Overcoming Self-Forgiveness Barriers

When psychologists point to barriers to self-forgiveness, the feeling of shame is a big one (Fisher and Exline 2010; Tangney and Dearing 2002). Although sometimes used synonymously, shame and guilt are different. Shame is an emotion that involves condemnation of the whole self and involves feeling small, powerless, exposed, and worthless. With shame, people focus on themselves and become isolated from others. Guilt is somewhat different. Although it's also a difficult emotion, guilt can motivate people to make amends for bad behavior rather than stay focused on their own perceived worthlessness and misery. As Fisher and Exline (2010) note, "If one feels guilt about a specific action, one can alleviate the guilt through reparations and amends; but if one feels shame, it is difficult to make up for a global sense of being a bad person" (551).

The self-forgiveness process requires diligence. You need to know you're worth all of this work and effort. You deserve the peace that comes from forgiving yourself! If you don't truly believe this, self-forgiveness will be elusive. The products of self-forgiveness are self-acceptance, and goodwill toward and reconciliation with the self. If you don't feel worthy of these outcomes, then working toward them won't be very productive.

When you did exercise 3.5, you considered how you are more than just your behavior. Making mistakes doesn't make you a bad person. To overcome shame as an obstacle to self-forgiveness, flex that self-compassion muscle. Think of what your compassionate other would say about your misdeeds, and practice self-kindness as you work through this process. Also, a little humility will go a long way. Humility is more than being modest or self-effacing; it's the capacity to be able to see both your strengths and weaknesses accurately without being defensive (Exline et al. 2004). Doesn't that remind you of the clarity that comes from mindfulness? If you've completed the exercises in previous chapters and have an authentic willingness to move forward, you have a good foundation for the hard but worthwhile work of self-forgiveness.

STEPS TOWARD SELF-FORGIVENESS

This section outlines steps you can undertake to work toward self-forgiveness, but this isn't a neat step-by-step procedure that can be followed like a recipe for making fudge (or snickerdoodle cookies). Some parts of the process overlap, and you may return to some of these steps over and over again as you work toward self-forgiveness in different areas of your life.

These steps toward self-forgiveness draw on the collective works of Robert Enright (1996), Everett Worthington, Jr. (2013), Paul Mauger et al. (1992), Mickie Fisher and Julie Exline (2006, 2010), and Margaret Holmgren (1998, 2002) as well as on principles from twelve-step traditions. They are as follows: acknowledging an objective interpersonal transgression; taking responsibility for your role in committing the offense; observing and processing negative emotions triggered by the act; thinking about the offense from a broader perspective; making amends; and making meaning and moving forward.

Step 1: Acknowledging an Objective Interpersonal Transgression

Think about something you said or did during your marriage or divorce that was hurtful. We realize this is asking you to dredge up something painful that you'd probably prefer not to think about. We wish there were an easier way, but to achieve authentic self-forgiveness, you've got to acknowledge your mistakes. Try to identify a specific wrongdoing for which you've felt guilt or shame or both, and that you're having a difficult time dealing with. It's important that you focus on something that was hurtful to someone. In other words, it shouldn't be a figment of your inner critic's overactive imagination. Instead, your words or action should be something that an outside observer looking at the situation objectively would acknowledge as hurtful. For example, Cara might focus on her drunk-driving arrest. This behavior hurt Gary, her parents, her employer, her patients, and herself, and they put others' lives at risk—an outside observer could easily see that. Use the following exercise to identify an interpersonal offense that you'll focus on for the rest of the chapter.

EXERCISE 6.2: Identifying Your Hurtful Mistakes

GOAL   The goal of this exercise is to identify an interpersonal offense related to your divorce for which you'd like to forgive yourself and which will serve as the primary focus of your work for the other exercises in this chapter.

INSTRUCTIONS   Take a moment to think and write as objectively as possible about the interpersonal offense that you'll be working on throughout this chapter.

KEEP IN MIND   Humility will come in handy when you do this exercise. Don't give in to your inner critic's tendency to exaggerate, but don't allow yourself to sugarcoat events either. This can be tough—a good dose of self-compassion will help this exercise go down much more smoothly.

DESCRIPTION   Describe the offense.

_____

_____

_____

_____

_____

_____

_____

_____

REFLECTION   What was it like to acknowledge your hurtful actions? You'll return to these feelings in a subsequent exercise.

_____

_____

_____

_____

_____

Well done! You've taken the first step. Now it's time to examine your role in the hurt experienced by the other person.

Step 2: Taking Responsibility

In seeking self-forgiveness for your actions, keep in mind the differences between authentic and pseudo self-forgiveness. Remember? It basically boils down to taking responsibility for your role in the hurtful event. But that doesn't mean that you accept all of the responsibility for what happened; you accept only the part that belongs to you.

Again, it will help to look at Cara's case. To be accountable for her arrest, Cara must own up to the fact that she chose to drink and then got behind the wheel of her car. She alone made that decision. Immediately after the event, Cara blamed her friend, who was supposed to be the designated driver but didn't follow through, but as she has begun to practice mindfulness and humility, she's been able to see her own role in the situation. While she owns up to the fact that her actions hurt her parents, she doesn't take full responsibility for her father's sense of public humiliation for having to bail her out of jail. Since the incident, he has continued to bring up this topic and won't let it go. This has more to do with her father and how he's able to deal with these events than with Cara. Cara is practicing humility through her attempt to clearly see what she's responsible for and what isn't hers to own.

The next exercise invites you to look at your role in the situation you described in exercise 6.2.

EXERCISE 6.3: Taking Responsibility

GOAL   The goal of this exercise is to take responsibility for the hurt you caused.

INSTRUCTIONS   Go back to exercise 6.2 and read your description of what you did to cause another person pain during your marriage or the divorce process. The rest of the exercise will refer to that event. To ensure that you're neither shirking your responsibility nor taking on too much, consider discussing this exercise with your therapist or someone else who will give you honest feedback. Remember to be kind to yourself—we all make mistakes.

QUESTIONS   As best you can, describe the hurt experienced by the person who was affected by your actions.

_____

_____

_____

_____

_____

Now think about your role in causing this hurt. What aspects of this person's pain directly resulted from what you did?

_____

_____

_____

_____

What aspects of this person's pain may be less connected to your actions?

_____

_____

_____

_____

REFLECTION   Now that you've clarified your responsibility in this situation, write down some words that describe your emotional state. You'll return to these feelings in a subsequent exercise.

_____

_____

_____

_____

_____

What sort of words did you use to describe your emotional state? If most of them are negative or difficult, you're in good company. While doing this exercise, people usually list difficult emotional states. The next exercise provides a framework to help you move through these tough feelings.

Step 3: Observing and Processing Negative Emotions

An important part of the self-forgiveness process is allowing yourself to acknowledge and sit with the negative emotions that occur as a result of taking responsibility for your actions. In chapter 3, we referred to the commonly cited equation *pain x resistance = suffering*. This expression suggests that the more you wish away, avoid, or struggle with painful emotions, the more you are likely to suffer. Suffering generally comes when you're in a painful situation and you invest much of your energy in comparing your harsh reality to some ideal. You not only experience your pain but add to your misery by telling yourself that things should be better. Psychologist Albert Ellis called this type of thinking *should-ing on yourself*. (Try not to should on yourself or others!)

Think about what you've learned about painful emotions so far in this book: they're an inevitable part of life, they don't last forever, and when you touch them with your awareness, their power diminishes. So what can you do to process these difficult emotions without wallowing in them or avoiding them all together?

EXERCISE 6.4: Becoming an OWNER of Your Difficult Emotions

GOAL   The goal of this exercise is to help you acknowledge and process difficult emotions as you work toward self-forgiveness.

INSTRUCTION   Go back to the reflection sections of exercises 6.2 and 6.3, and note the negative emotions that you listed. Answer the following questions about your experience with those feelings.

KEEP IN MIND   Remind yourself this is a necessary part of the process. You're not alone in your feelings. Everyone who's doing this important work feels guilt, sadness, and a host of other painful emotions in the process. Try not to get discouraged, and hang in there!

QUESTIONS   When you experience these feelings, what is your typical response? For example, do you acknowledge and stay with them, distract yourself, beat yourself up for having the feelings in the first place, or do something else?

_____

_____

_____

_____

If you're usually able to stay with the feelings without judging them or pushing them away, keep up the good work! You're well on your way to processing the difficult emotional by-products of moving toward self-forgiveness. If you most often avoid painful feelings, try these next suggestions. We've developed an acronym—OWNER—to help you own and be with these difficult emotions.

O: Open your awareness to the difficult emotions that come from taking responsibility for your actions. Try not to avoid them.

W: Where do you feel the emotion? For example, does it manifest somewhere in your body?

N: Name the feeling. Is it sadness, fear, hurt, anger, regret, guilt, or something else?

E: Embrace the feeling even though this may be difficult. Welcome it as a visitor that won't likely stay long. Comfort yourself by acknowledging that it will pass.

R: Resist the temptation to evaluate your experience as either good or bad. In a self-compassionate and nonjudgmental way, just allow the emotional experience to be.

The next time a negative emotion surrounding the offense surfaces, be an OWNER: use these strategies to process and be with your feelings.

REFLECTION   After you have tried this, reflect on a time in the past when you used one or more of the OWNER strategies. Write about the experience here.

_____

_____

_____

_____

_____

_____

_____

_____

_____

Now that you've taken some time to process these difficult feelings, it will help to put all of this in context.

Step 4: Putting What Happened into a Broader Perspective

Authentic self-forgiveness entails understanding that "each person is part of a community of imperfect others who are mostly striving to be the best people they can be" (Jacinto and Edwards 2011, 429). That's not to say that being part of the imperfect human race automatically excuses you for your mistakes. Rather, if you put your actions into a broader perspective, you're more likely to make amends and connect to others and be less likely to isolate yourself and hide in your shame. Part of this process involves understanding that all of us have attitudes and behavior patterns that can lead us to hurt others, either accidentally or purposefully. While such shortcomings may very well have worked to get your needs met in the past, they can turn into dysfunctional patterns if you don't have self-awareness. (This perspective may be somewhat familiar if you are acquainted with twelve-step programs, such as Alcoholics Anonymous.)

Authentic self-forgiveness involves identifying behavior patterns that got you into trouble in the first place, so you don't do the same thing in the future. Margaret Holmgren (1998) notes that people "should not self-forgive and forget" (78). Not forgetting doesn't mean holding a grudge against yourself for committing the wrong. It means that as you work toward change, you need to be aware of your tendency to engage in these problematic behaviors and attitudes so that you don't continue to hurt others.

Cara, for example, is fiercely independent and detests asking for help. That quality served her well growing up, but when she needed assistance to stop drinking, she wouldn't allow herself to reach out. Her resistance to seeking help was one of the factors that led to a drunk-driving offense. Another behavior pattern that got her into trouble was attention seeking. Cara validated her self-worth through the attention she received from others, particularly men. Although this seemed to work for her when she was younger, this behavior stopped getting the type of results she wanted and eventually backfired. How about you? What attitudes and behavior patterns contributed to the transgression for which you're seeking self-forgiveness?

EXERCISE 6.5: Identifying and Letting Go of Negative Attitudes and Behavior Patterns

GOAL   The goal of this exercise is to help you identify the attitudes and behavior patterns that contributed to the hurt you have caused others.

INSTRUCTIONS   Think about what attitude or behavioral patterns contributed to your hurtful actions. Fear of change, perfectionism, a tendency to focus too much on your own needs, a need to control people or circumstances, and dishonesty are some examples of potentially hurtful attitudes or behavioral patterns.

KEEP IN MIND   As always, remember your self-compassion skills while you do this work.

QUESTIONS   Name an attitude or behavioral pattern that contributed to your hurtful actions. If you can think of more than one, list them here.

Example 1: *I tend to be a people pleaser.*

Example 2: *I often take care of the needs of others but neglect my own.*

_____

_____

When and how has this attitude or behavioral pattern been beneficial to you?

_____

_____

_____

_____

When has it harmed you or others?

_____

_____

_____

_____

Do you know others who exhibit this pattern? How have their behaviors or attitudes affected you?

_____

_____

_____

_____

REFLECTION   How might letting go of this negative pattern benefit you and others?

_____

_____

_____

_____

_____

_____

_____

By identifying and making a commitment to change your shortcomings, you are demonstrating respect for yourself and the person that you've harmed in the context of your divorce. You're laying the groundwork for real and lasting personal growth. This sets the stage for making amends, which is addressed in the next step.

Step 5: Making Amends

One of the distinctions between pseudo and authentic self-forgiveness is how much effort you put into it (Fisher and Exline 2006), and it's in this step, making amends, that you can really see that difference. You've already done some important work on yourself. You've taken responsibility for your hurtful behavior, sat with the difficult feelings that came as a result, and taken a good, hard look at long-standing behavior patterns that contributed to your misdeed. We hope this work has helped to change your heart and mind about the mistake. Now we're going to ask you to do some interpersonal work; this is where you get to walk the talk.

Making amends can involve restitution to the person (or people) that you've harmed. Through these actions, you're able to bring closure to the episode and demonstrate that you've done all you can do to repair the damage. This facilitates self-forgiveness and has the potential to heal not only your heart but your damaged relationships as well. In the twelve-step tradition, making direct amends is strongly encouraged unless doing so would produce more harm than good. This may take the form of an apology, some sort of restitution, or something else that directly involves the person who was wronged. But if you decide to make direct amends, be careful about any expectations you might have. You don't know how your attempt to set things right will be received, so not having any expectations about the outcome is important.

Sometimes it's not possible to make direct amends. For example, you may have no contact with the wronged party, or approaching that person (or people) may be inappropriate or make matters worse. Under those conditions, you can make a positive difference by correcting your behavior to decrease the likelihood that you'll commit the same wrong in the future.

For example, Cara has felt significant guilt about the double life she lived online and in bars at the end of her marriage. Although she tried to directly apologize to Gary (he speaks to her only through his attorney) and is no longer unfaithful to a romantic partner, she felt the need to do something more to facilitate her self-forgiveness and attempt to right this wrong. As a result, Cara decided to volunteer with an agency that serves people with disabilities. Gary's brother, whom Gary loved dearly, had a disability and died not long after Cara and Gary were married. Cara feels this is a way to make indirect restitution to Gary.

If you are considering making an indirect amend, you need to make sure that you aren't trying to dodge a direct amend out of fear or embarrassment. If a direct apology or an offering of restitution will cause no further harm, you are likely to grow more from making one than from making an indirect amend. You need to judge for yourself what will best lead you down the path toward self-forgiveness. The next exercise will help you explore this step of the process.

EXERCISE 6.6: Making Amends

GOAL The goal of this exercise is to help you identify repentant behaviors that will facilitate self-forgiveness.

INSTRUCTIONS Draw upon your creativity to complete this exercise. You may need to think outside the box to identify something you can do to make amends. What you choose to do will depend on the circumstances of your offense.

KEEP IN MIND As you think about what you will do to make amends, be reasonable with yourself. If you feel shame or considerable guilt, you may try to do too much in an attempt to make up for the mistake. It may help to discuss your ideas with someone you trust for perspective.

QUESTIONS For the hurtful behavior on which you have previously focused, is a direct apology possible or appropriate? Why or why not?

_____

_____

_____

_____

If it is possible, how will the benefits of a direct apology outweigh the costs associated with not directly apologizing?

_____

_____

_____

_____

If a direct apology is inappropriate, what can you do to make amends? How might you make indirect restitution?

_____

_____

_____

_____

Describe your plan to make amends (either with or without a direct apology). Then act on it.

_____

_____

_____

_____

REFLECTION   What was the outcome of your attempt at amends? How do you feel about the progress you've made toward self-forgiveness?

_____

_____

_____

_____

_____

_____

_____

_____

Congratulations! You've done some hard and significant work. You're well on your way to developing a self-forgiving orientation that will serve you well in the future.

Step 6: Making Meaning and Moving Forward

Moving through the self-forgiveness process has a way of shedding new light on the hurt you've caused others and its aftermath. This chapter will end the same way it began by reminding you that occasionally we all do things, either accidentally or purposefully, that hurt others. The important thing is how you handle it with those you've hurt as well as in your own heart and mind. The lessons you learn and the meaning you make from the pain that you and others experience can lay the foundation for significant personal growth, if you're willing to do the work to put it in perspective.

WHAT'S NEXT?

How can you make meaning of your suffering? In the next chapter, we'll discuss how the stories you tell yourself about the ups and downs of your life have the capacity to either worsen or alleviate the inevitable suffering that is part of the human experience. We provide strategies to help you find meaning in both the peaks and valleys associated with your divorce, which will help to promote peace of mind and lasting happiness.

CHAPTER 7

"How Do I Make Sense of All This?"

Finding Meaning

Following a divorce, your assumptions about life are challenged, and you may be prompted to think, *Why me? Why did this happen? What does my life mean now?* Human beings are meaning-making machines. Viktor Frankl (1946), a psychiatrist and Holocaust survivor, claimed that the search for meaning is the primary human motivation. We all try to make sense of what happens to us so that our lives have coherence and predictability. Finding meaning when the going gets tough may help you through the hard times and also can be a vehicle for growth so that you're even better off than before the hardship. This might be hard to hear when you're suffering, but it's true. Come on—let's make some sweet meaning together!

Chapter Focus

This chapter provides evidence that finding meaning in your divorce can promote growth and adaptability. It also provides some strategies to help you explore new ways to find meaning in your divorce experience.

LOOKING FOR MEANING

No doubt about it, life can be messy. Sometimes it feels like whoever is running this cosmic show has one twisted sense of humor, because weird—and often painful—circumstances seem to come out of nowhere when you least expect it. Sometimes stuff happens that defies explanation. Despite careful planning and the best of intentions, it all goes wonky, anyway. It's as though the proverbial you-know-what hits the fan when you didn't even know the stupid fan had been turned on in the first place!

Learning how to make sense out of life's struggles can be important to your health and well-being. Finding meaning is a way of connecting events, experiences, and relationships in a way that makes sense to you, the individual meaning-maker (Baumeister 1991). Making meaning is like writing your life story as a coherent narrative in which the past, the present, and even the future are woven together in a way that makes sense. Although the meaning you assign to your life events can be influenced by messages that you get from the larger culture and your family, you're ultimately the sole author of your life narrative.

WHAT MAKING MEANING MEANS

Psychologists Crystal Park and Susan Folkman (1997) describe meaning as having two different components. Each person develops what they call *global meaning*, which is a broad view of the world that includes your general beliefs, goals, and feelings. This overall meaning is developed throughout your lifetime. For example, you develop beliefs about the fairness and predictability of life, goals related to your relationships and successes, and feelings of purpose. When a stressful situation occurs, you also give it a meaning (known as *situational meaning*). If the meaning you assign to a specific event is different from how you look at life overall, you try to make sense of what happened. The bigger this difference or discrepancy in these two types of meaning, the more you rev the engine in your meaning-making machine.

For example, one component of your global meaning is how you understand the concept of family and relationships among family members. When your divorce occurred, you assigned that event a specific (or situational) meaning. Furthermore, the degree of difference between what family meant before the divorce and what it means afterward is related to how much distress you're experiencing. Distress can fuel your motivation to reduce the discrepancy between these two types of meaning.

This meaning-making process has both thinking and feeling components, and there's no one correct way to make meaning. People can reevaluate their global meanings, change how they view the specific situation, or do a little of both. Other strategies can include changing your goals and reconsidering your sense of purpose (Park 2010).

The next exercise will help you take a closer look at how you've begun to make meaning out of family now that you're separated or divorced. This may not be a particular challenge for you, but our experience working with folks who are going through divorce suggests that this is one area in which people often struggle. Even if this isn't an area that causes you distress, completing the exercise can help you better understand your own personal meaning-making process.

EXERCISE 7.1: Making Meaning Out of Family

GOAL   The goal of this exercise is to help you better understand how you make meaning out of family.

INSTRUCTIONS   This exercise has three parts: a description of how you defined family before your divorce, a description of how you define family now that you're divorced, and a reflection on how you came to your current definition.

Part 1   How did you define family before your divorce?

_____

_____

_____

Part 2   How do you define family now?

_____

_____

_____

REFLECTION   How did you come to the definition of family that you had before the divorce? In other words, were you raised with this idea in your family of origin, did you get messages from the media about what family meant, or are there other sources that contributed to your meaning of family?

_____

_____

_____

Did your definition of family change after the divorce? Why or why not?

_____

_____

_____

If your definition of family has changed, how did you arrive at your new definition?

_____

_____

_____

_____

Family can be defined in many ways, but what's important is that your definition makes sense to you. Many people are brought up with the conventional notion that a family is defined as a mom, a dad, and their children. Others include relatives such as grandparents, aunts, uncles, and cousins in their definition of family. Still others think of family as those with whom you share a close bond—a group of people who are interdependent and committed to one another—regardless of whether you are related by blood, marriage, or adoption. Given the current rates of divorce, the notion of family is a fluid one, and making sense out of it requires emotional and cognitive flexibility.

Coming to terms with what family means is just one area in which you'll be challenged during your quest for meaning postdivorce. You may be struggling to make sense out of altered life goals or find yourself reevaluating life's purpose. You may be dealing with spiritual questions. In upcoming pages, we'll help you focus on three areas in which divorced people often struggle to make meaning: reconceptualizing your identity, redefining the relationship with your ex, and exploring life lessons thrown your way on this divorce odyssey. Before moving ahead, we want to distinguish between the process and outcome of meaning making and look at how each relates to your postdivorce adjustment and well-being.

Making Meaning: The Process

Attempts at making meaning are not always helpful in reducing distress (Park 2010). Although there's no prescribed timetable or scorecard for when you've made your meaning (we envision five judges with stopwatches holding up cardboard numbers between 1 and 10), it's pretty clear that continued rumination and intrusive thoughts that cause significant and ongoing distress promote neither positive adjustment nor a sense of well-being.

When a situation seems to defy explanation, however, rumination and intrusive thoughts can occur, and no amount of mental gymnastics gets you closer to understanding. This is when the skills you've been working on—mindfulness (see chapter 2) and self-compassion (see chapter 3)—can come to the rescue. When the troublesome *why* thoughts come, you can bring a nonjudgmental awareness to them and treat yourself with loving-kindness and compassion. When you do this, these thoughts will lose their power, and you'll be less likely to ruminate and be carried away by the thought stream.

If you've been doing the exercises in this book all along, you know that practicing mindfulness and self-compassion is a process that takes time. In your mindfulness practice, it's likely that you'll kindly notice these intrusive thoughts hundreds of times. But the more you do, the less space they'll take up in your heart and mind. Don't push them away—notice them and let them go. The more you let go of these thoughts, the more likely you will be to come to a place of acceptance—which is one way to make meaning of things that defy explanation.

Finally, meaning making is an ongoing process that involves connecting the dots from the past, present, and the future. This means that what doesn't make sense today may be more comprehensible down the road. It's possible that you haven't yet discovered that piece of the puzzle that can make the picture complete for you. Who knows, maybe that puzzle piece is an event or experience that hasn't even happened yet! If you've got at least one troublesome question for which you have been searching for answers, the following exercise can help you let go of it and cultivate acceptance.

EXERCISE 7.2: Letting Go and Working Toward Acceptance

GOAL   The goal of this exercise is to help you let go of distressing questions about your divorce that, at this point, seem inexplicable.

INSTRUCTIONS   Focus on one question about your divorce that seems to defy explanation, and causes rumination and intrusive thoughts. In other words, select a question that is distressing to you and that you've tried and failed to answer.

For example, some divorced folks wrestle with the issue of infidelity and question why their spouse was unfaithful. Others wonder why their spouse fell out of love with them. After you've identified the question, consider your reactions to the question and then develop a ritual to help you let go of it and the troubling emotions it prompts.

QUESTIONS   Write down the distressing question here.

_____

_____

List the emotions that come up when you think about this question.

_____

_____

What have you done in the past when these emotions surfaced?

_____

_____

What skills can you utilize to decrease your resistance to these emotions? Drawing on the skills you've learned in previous chapters, write down a plan that will help you let go and accept the emotions prompted by the question. For example, you might consider strategies related to mindfulness, self-compassion, or acceptance.

_____

_____

_____

_____

RITUAL   Sometimes it can be helpful to develop a ritual or a symbolic action that can help you let go of troubling questions and emotions. Some people write their questions down and ceremoniously tear or burn them up. One client we worked with took a spiritual perspective. He wrote down his troubling questions and placed them in a box. He explained that by putting the questions in the box, he gave them over to God and trusted that if the question needed an answer, it would come when he was ready for it. What ritual can you devise to help you let go of these inexplicable questions?

_____

_____

_____

Although the meaning-making process may not always bring about immediate clarity, when things make sense, the result is a feeling of comfort and coherence. That's why we're all so motivated to search for meaning. The next section discusses some of the positive outcomes that can occur when meanings are made.

Meanings Made: The Outcome

People can experience well-being and enhanced adjustment after making meaning of difficult or traumatic events (Park 2010). For example, compared to how they saw themselves before the hardship, people may perceive themselves as stronger, more sensitive to others, and more open to accepting help and support (Tedeschi and Calhoun 1996). They may change their life priorities in new and beneficial ways or have an increased appreciation for life and relationships. One study found that a concrete sense of meaning was related to psychological well-being after separation and divorce (Bevvino and Sharkin 2003).

However, not all meanings are made equal. Some people's global meaning narrative includes a malevolent world populated by people waiting to take advantage of them or break their hearts. For those who are writing a narrative like this, things aren't supposed to go smoothly, and if they do, it's a total surprise. There is preliminary evidence that individuals with gloomy global meanings are more likely to experience poor adjustment (Park 2010).

The positive psychology research on which we base this book shows that forgiveness, self-compassion, connectedness, and optimism are associated with well-being. Based on this evidence, it would seem that people who construct a hopeful narrative characterized by these positive qualities are more likely to lead happy and contented lives than people who focus on a story of fear and separation. The best part of all of this meaningful meaning stuff is that you alone are the one who weaves together the tale of your life. So what kind of story are you going to write?

FINDING NEW MEANING AFTER DIVORCE

Life course theorists, such as social worker Elizabeth Hutchison (2005), think of divorce as a life transition, an identifiable event that produces a shift in your status and roles. A transition marks the ending of an old phase of life and the beginning of a new one. Transitions produce changes in your life trajectories. You can think of a life trajectory as the direction of an aspect of your life. For example, people may have a family life trajectory, an educational trajectory, and a career trajectory. These trajectories are interdependent and overlap.

Your divorce has changed your family life trajectory, and it's probably had an impact on other areas of your life too. You are in transition now, and with so much change, there's a lot for you to make meaning about.

Rethinking Your Identity

Divorce means not only the loss of your spouse from your day-to-day life but also a new lifestyle and way of being. These external changes prompt shifts in your identity and how you see yourself in relation to the world. Such shifts in identity are common after such a big life transition like divorce, and the degree and nature of the shift can depend on many different factors. For example, did you or your partner initiate the divorce? Are you a man or a woman? Do you have children, and if so, where do they live? Did your divorce require you to move from the community where you lived while married? Did your job status change after the divorce?

People who are divorced are often faced with the challenge of having to perform tasks that their partner used to do. This can include, but certainly is not limited to, things like doing the laundry, cooking, fixing the car, mowing the lawn, and taking care of finances. Taking on these things by yourself requires independence and oftentimes courage. One of our clients talked about how her husband did the repair work around the house, and after their separation, she was faced with the daunting challenge of fixing things by herself. When it came time to paint the mailbox post, she was doubtful of her ability. Then, she had an epiphany—what's the worst that could happen? Her paint job would suck? Big deal! So, she painted the post. As a result, the mailbox looked awesome and she was motivated to take other risks. Thus, divorce can provide an opportunity for you to develop new abilities and personal strengths.

Divorce can also give you a chance to cultivate new interests or do things you always wanted to do but didn't because of your spouse. Another client began hiking and eventually joined an outdoor club, something his ex-wife would never do. As a result, being an outdoorsman has become a big part of his identity. Another way of incorporating a new aspect of your identity is to make physical changes. Some folks change their hairstyle or begin an exercise program after they divorce.

A woman with whom Crystal worked took her wedding jewelry and had it redesigned into a beautiful new ring and set of spectacular earrings. She used her engagement diamond for one of the earrings and bought another stone to match. This newfangled jewelry represented something old and something new, which both acknowledged the importance of her past and the bright new life path she was traveling. This client also acknowledged that it took time and effort to get to this place of acceptance and meaning, but every step she took was worth it.

So, how about you? Take a look at some of the external changes that have happened as a result of your divorce and how they've influenced your identity. Remember that you can choose your new identity—you're the meaning maker after all!

EXERCISE 7.3: Exploring Your New Identity

GOAL The goal of this exercise is to help you think creatively and constructively about your new postdivorce identity.

INSTRUCTIONS   This exercise has three parts. You'll be examining what external changes have occurred since your divorce, some of the new qualities you've realized in yourself, and interests you'd like to cultivate that complement your new and evolving identity. Try to focus on your strengths and abilities in this exercise. In your new life, you'll be building on those capacities to promote your happiness and well-being.

Part 1   Describe five external changes that have occurred as a result of your divorce. This can include where you live, whom you live with, your job status, and so on.

1. _____

_____

2. _____

_____

3. _____

_____

4. _____

_____

5. _____

_____

Part 2   Name five positive qualities or traits that you've either discovered or developed more fully as a result of your divorce and these external changes. For example, some people discover their independence, courage, or ability to nurture.

1. _____

_____

2. _____

_____

3. _____

_____

4. _____

_____

5. _____

_____

Part 3   What are five interests or activities that you'd like to explore now that you're divorced?

1. _____

_____

2. _____

_____

3. _____

_____

4. _____

_____

5. _____

_____

REFLECTION   Putting this all together, what do you come up with? Say you were going to advertise your new identity in a best-selling magazine that we'll call *Identity Today*. The goal of the ad is to declare your new identity to the world. (Not to attract anyone romantically—this isn't an eHarmony profile.) Based on your responses in parts 1, 2, and 3, write an identity ad describing the new you.

_____

_____

_____

_____

_____

_____

Here's to the new you! Given that you are growing and changing, your relationships with others are bound to morph as well. We would guess that the toughest of these would be the one you have with your ex.

Redefining Your Relationship with Your Ex

Many people see marriage as a lifelong commitment. When their partnerships have dissolved, they often struggle with how to relate to their former life partners. In making meaning after divorce, it's helpful to spend time thinking about what role your ex will play in your life moving forward. Even if you never plan to interact with your ex again, that person will play a role in your memories and in the stories you tell about your divorce.

There's no simple formula for redefining your relationship with your ex. Many factors need to be considered, such as the circumstances surrounding your divorce, whether or not you have children, your ex's past and current behavior, and your own preferences. What follows are some different possibilities for how you could redefine this relationship. Remember that you can choose how you want to respond to your ex—that's something that's under your control.

YOUR EX AS A FRIEND

Some people wish to maintain a friendship with their ex after divorce. Crystal fondly remembers her dad's first wife coming to family Christmas and Thanksgiving dinners during her childhood. (He was on his third wife by then, but let's not go too far afield.)

However, this sort of relationship can work only if the level of acrimony has dropped, both parties are interested in maintaining a friendship, and there's no risk of physical or emotional abuse. Unless these conditions are met, trying to reconnect as friends will likely lead to more suffering. Simply put, remaining friends should be considered as an option only when it's in the best interest of everyone involved and it helps you come to terms with your divorce. Remaining friends may not be possible in the initial period following a divorce, but sometimes the passage of time and additional life experience opens up this door. Consider the case of Raj.

The Case of Raj

Raj, who is in his early sixties, had been married for over twenty-five years to his wife, Jasmine. For most of their married life, Jasmine complained about numerous physical and psychological problems, but she never sought help or took steps to improve her lot in life. They divorced when Raj realized that Jasmine was unlikely to change anytime soon and that his life with her had become unbearable. Eight years later, as a result of attending a workshop about forgiveness, he decided to reach out and give her a call. During the conversation, he learned that she was living alone and in ill health. One day he visited her and helped her with some things around the house. He was amazed at how his own anger and bitterness, which he had held on to for so many years, had begun to disappear. For the first time since his divorce, he wanted to be a part of her life again—this time as a compassionate friend.

Although reestablishing a friendship with an ex isn't possible or desirable in many cases, some folks find that it enriches their lives. For Raj, reconnecting with his ex helped him to make meaning of his divorce in positive ways. Raj's view of himself changed. He saw that he had a soft and compassionate heart, and was able to see how his ex was suffering. He no longer felt the need to avoid or condemn her.

YOUR EX AS A CO-PARENT

Does your ex have strengths as a parent? If so, what are they? If your ex has short-comings as a parent, don't forget that all parents do. As long as your ex is a reasonably competent parent, your kids will benefit from your willingness to work together on parenting. And if you've chosen to include forgiveness as part of your postdivorce narrative, it's less likely that your kids will get caught in the middle during disputes.

Part of your postdivorce narrative could include a chapter on collaborative co-parenting with your ex if that's a reasonable possibility. Collaborative co-parenting involves communicating regularly with your ex to discuss parenting and working together to make decisions that are in the best interests of your children. If collaborative co-parenting is an unrealistic goal given the state of your relationship with your ex, you might consider parallel parenting. Parallel parenting involves a minimal amount of communication with your ex. With parallel parenting, rules for children can differ at each household, and each parent agrees not to undermine the other parent's authority. With parallel parenting, there is less of a united front when it comes to setting rules and disciplining, but it is better for children than high-conflict parenting, in which children are frequently placed in the middle of heated arguments between parents.

YOUR EX AS [*FILL IN THE BLANK*]

How else might you redefine your relationship with your ex? If you saw your life as a screenplay, what role would you assign him or her?

EXERCISE 7.4: Redefining Your Ex's Role

GOAL   The goal of this exercise is to consider the role that your ex will have in your life moving forward.

INSTRUCTIONS   Movie scripts typically provide a brief description of each role, so the reader understands who is who. Similarly, we'd like for you to briefly describe in the left column the roles that you've assigned to your ex in the past that haven't proven helpful. In the right column, list new roles that you could assign to your ex to help you move on.

KEEP IN MIND   There are a few important factors to consider when redefining your relationship with your ex:

1. Is it safe to continue interacting with your ex?

2. Has your ex shown that he or she will treat you respectfully if you interact in the future?

3. What role would you like your ex to play in your divorce story or your life moving forward?

Old Role That Wasn't Helpful	New Role That Will Help You Move On
Example 1: *My ex was supposed to make me happy.*	*My ex taught me that happiness is found from within.*
Example 2: *My ex destroyed my life.*	*My ex's behavior challenged me to draw upon strengths that I never realized I had.*
Example 3: *My ex has no redeeming qualities.*	*My ex was a terrible spouse but is a loving parent, and together we can help our children adjust to the divorce with as little stress as possible.*
1.	
2.	
3.	
4.	
5.	

REFLECTION   Your willingness to question your old assumptions about your ex and focus on ways in which your painful experiences can help you grow as a person is a tremendous gift to yourself. You're transforming your life by drawing upon your inner strength. Take a moment to let that sink in.

Redefining your relationship with your ex is one way to make meaning of your life postdivorce. You also can find new meaning in life by identifying what you've learned from this relationship and from your divorce.

Identifying Life Lessons in Your Divorce Story

Some of the most important and meaningful things learned in life come with a high price. As someone who has just paid (probably both literally and metaphorically) some serious dues during your divorce, what have you learned? What can you use from the experience and your relationship with your ex to live more peacefully and happily now and in the future? We realize this is a deep question and one that will likely take some time to process. Be willing to take as much as you need.

In our work with people weathering the divorce storm, we've been struck by the positive transformation that occurs postdivorce among those willing to try new ways of thinking, be more open to their internal and external experiences, and connect with others for support. As time passes, they're often surprised by how graduating from the divorce school of hard knocks has made them more resilient and, ultimately, happier people. Here are some of the lessons that our clients have shared with us:

- *Actions by a romantic partner speak louder than words.*

- *My happiness can't come solely from my partner.*

- *I have more empathy for people who've been cheated on by a romantic partner.*

- *Reaching out to others for support during difficult times is a sign of strength. Going it alone merely serves my pride.*

- *Taking care of myself isn't selfish. I can't be fully present to care for others unless I take care of myself emotionally, physically, and spiritually.*

- *I deserve peace and happiness.*

- *I can't control everything that happens. I can only control my own reactions to life situations.*

We could go on and on, but instead we invite you to take a moment to consider what you have learned from the divorce process and your relationship with your ex.

EXERCISE 7.5: Lessons Learned in the Divorce Classroom

GOAL   The goal of this exercise is to reflect upon lessons that you've learned as a result of your relationship with your ex and as a result of the divorce.

INSTRUCTIONS   List the top five things that you've learned. Keep in mind that sometimes the most difficult circumstances (and people) provide the greatest learning opportunities.

LIST   The top five things you learned:

1. _____

_____

2. _____

_____

3. _____

_____

4. _____

_____

5. _____

_____

REFLECTION   Take a moment to think about how the lessons you've learned might help you in future relationships. Do you feel like a stronger and wiser person after having learned these lessons?

_____

_____

Sometimes life presents difficult situations that are like poorly wrapped gifts. They don't appear to contain anything good or desirable, but once you unwrap them, there are all sorts of goodies inside. So if you can get past the mangled bow, misshapen box, and ugly wrapping paper, something wonderful is likely to be uncovered.

WHAT'S NEXT?

The next chapter will take a look at how adopting an attitude of gratitude can help with postdivorce adjustment. Speaking of gratitude, we're so thankful you're on this journey with us!

CHAPTER 8

"Nothing Seems to Be Going Right"

Searching for Hidden Blessings

After all of the heartache, change, and uncertainty you've faced related to your divorce, it's not surprising if you sometimes feel the need to complain. In fact, complaining (especially about your ex) is a time-honored tradition among many divorced folks. How often have you or a divorced friend started a conversation with "You won't believe what my ex did this time…"?

Complaining about your problems may serve a function, but after a point it can become problematic. How do you know if your complaining has gotten out of hand? Can you learn to focus on the blessings in your life rather than on what's going wrong?

Chapter Focus

This chapter invites you to examine how strengthening your attitude of gratitude can help you cope with your divorce. We begin with a look at complaining and what function it may serve in your life. This is followed by an overview of recent scientific findings on the benefits of gratitude. Finally, we provide some practical suggestions for enhancing gratitude in your life.

RECOGNIZING YOUR INNER COMPLAINER

Talking about your struggles with someone you trust can be extraordinarily helpful. Folks often feel better knowing that there's someone willing to listen and provide support, even when solutions to problems are not immediately apparent. Complaining, on the other hand, is often counterproductive. There's a fine line between constructively processing feelings and complaining. How can you tell when you've crossed it?

As former United States Supreme Court Justice Potter Stewart famously said (about an entirely different topic), "I know it when I see it." It's easy to recognize complaining when you see it in others. It's much harder to spot complaining when you yourself are the complainer. Here are some clues to watch for:

- You're talking too much about problems related to your divorce and not enough about other topics.

- You're discussing your struggles with people who aren't well equipped to handle them, such as your kids, people you just met, the mail carrier.

- People start to avoid you or change the subject quickly whenever you start talking about your divorce.

- You're getting tired of thinking about or talking about your divorce.

If any or all of this sounds familiar to you, then your inner complainer may be getting the upper hand. You can do something about it.

CONFRONTING YOUR INNER COMPLAINER

Complaining is a choice, not an automatic and uncontrollable response to difficult circumstances. Indeed, some of us let our inner complainer take over prime-time programming in our lives. Have you ever known someone with a remarkable gift for finding something to complain about in every circumstance? Consider this story (original source unknown):

There was a mountain monastery that demanded a strict vow of silence from the monks. An exception was that once a year each monk could stand in front of the monastic community and say one word. After his first year, one monk stood up in front of the others and in a clear voice said, "The." He returned to his seat and began another year of silent retreat. After the second year had passed, the monk came before the group and said, "Food." Once again, he took his seat to resume his silent retreat. At the end of the third year, the monk addressed the group and said, "Stinks." There was an awkward silence. Finally, the abbot turned to the monk and said, "Look, you've been here three years, and all you do is complain!"

Like the monk, do you find yourself complaining all the time? Admittedly, the monk may have had a point. Maybe the food was awful and he was doing everyone a favor by speaking out. Perhaps the chef needed to hear the hard, cold truth about his poor cooking. Nevertheless, the fact remains that the monk complained whenever he opened his mouth.

Examining Why You Complain

If you find yourself complaining more often than you'd like, don't be too hard on yourself. The truth is we all have an inner complainer who wants to be heard from time to time. Instead of judging your inner complainer, it can be helpful to examine some of the reasons why you complain in the first place. Here are some possibilities.

You want others to know that you're suffering. If you're going through a difficult time, it's only natural to want others to understand what you're going through. Complaining is one way of communicating about your experiences and may be an attempt to feel less alone. You also hope that other people will agree with your perception of events and recognize how hard things have been. When others agree with your perceptions, you feel that your perspective and actions are justified.

You bond with others with similar experiences. How much time do your divorced friends spend complaining about their exes? Complaining is one way that divorced friends bond over shared experiences. However, when others are complaining about their exes, there can be pressure to join in. Have you ever found yourself complaining about your ex—not because you want to, but because everyone around you is doing so?

You want something to change. Sometimes you may complain because you hope that something will change. The monk at the monastery may have complained about the food because he hoped the chef would make improvements. Whether or not change occurs following a complaint depends on the circumstances and how you frame the complaint. However, complaining about your ex to a third party usually fails to bring about change. Complaining directly to your ex can makes things worse, particularly if the relationship is already acrimonious. If your ex didn't respond to complaints when you were married, any motivation to change is probably even lower now that the marriage has ended.

Complaining has become a habit. You may complain out of habit. In this case, you've allowed your inner complainer so much freedom that it takes over without your conscious awareness and shifts into autopilot.

EXERCISE 8.1: Getting in Touch with Your Inner Complainer

GOAL   The goal of this exercise is to take an honest look at your inner complainer.

INSTRUCTIONS   Answer the questions that follow about the role that complaining has in your life.

KEEP IN MIND   The purpose of this exercise is not to judge yourself harshly. Instead, in the spirit of mindfulness (see chapter 2) and self-compassion (see chapter 3), we invite you to become more aware of the function that complaining serves for you.

EXAMINING YOUR INNER COMPLAINER   On the following scale of 1 to 4, place an X next to the statement that best corresponds with your assessment of how often you complain, regardless of whether or not you voice these complaints to others. Complaints can be in your thoughts even if they aren't the focus of your conversations.

_____ 1. *I never complain. Complaining is not part of how I've approached my life since my divorce.*

_____ 2. *I complain every once in a while.*

_____ 3. *I find myself complaining more often than I'd like.*

_____ 4. *I've perfected the art of complaining and can complain with the best of them. Too bad complaining isn't a competitive sport, because I'd win the trophy. Then, I'd complain that the trophy wasn't nice enough.*

REASONS BEHIND YOUR COMPLAINING   Take a few moments to write down some of the reasons you complain. If you're having trouble coming up with reasons, consider some of the possibilities discussed in this chapter.

_____

_____

_____

_____

_____

ALTERNATIVES TO COMPLAINING   Can you think of more effective ways to get your needs met than complaining? If so, write them down in the space provided.

_____

_____

_____

_____

REFLECTION   You may not be aware of how often you complain. Consider checking with close friends or family members who would be willing to give you honest feedback. Find out if their observations about how often you complain are consistent with your perception. Also, in your mindfulness practice (see chapter 2), take notice of how often your thoughts focus on complaints, even if you don't voice them.

The Dark Side of Complaining

Under the right conditions, complaining can help to bring about constructive change, but it also has its dark side. Complaining becomes problematic when it becomes a major focus of your life. Think for a moment about someone you know who complains frequently. Do they seem happy? Are they fun to be around? Complaining has many disadvantages.

Complaining pushes others away. People who complain a lot bring a storm cloud with them wherever they go. As with bad weather, everyone in the vicinity is affected, and many may seek shelter. For instance, upon first dating again following a divorce, some folks complain so much about their ex that they inadvertently push their new romantic partner away.

Complaining contributes to negative mood. If you've been feeling depressed and you tend to view the events in your life through dark and gloomy glasses, complaining won't help. In fact, complaining will reinforce negative thoughts that contribute to your dark mood.

Complaining can keep you from changing your perspective. One of the secrets to emotional healing following a divorce is learning how to transform your perspective. Complaining reinforces a negative narrative about your life that keeps you stuck in your suffering.

Complaining can be a substitute for action. Complaining can give the false sense that you are doing something about your problems. However, while complaining can lead to constructive change under some circumstances, most complaining doesn't change the nature of the problem.

Complaining can negatively impact your kids. Divorced parents sometimes find themselves complaining about their ex to their kids. This can be very painful for children to hear. Even if you aren't complaining directly about your ex, complaining could have a negative impact on the kids' moods. Besides, children can learn how to become good complainers from their parents.

Giving Your Inner Complainer a Rest

Is your inner complainer wearing out you and others? Is it time to give your inner complainer a rest? If the answer to these questions is no, and you're not ready to give up complaining, that's understandable. After all, you've been through some really difficult experiences. In fact, if you want to complain about our decision to include a section in this book about complaining, that's okay with us. (We'll be the first to admit that we complain sometimes.)

However, if you want to spend less time listening to your inner complainer, consider scheduling fifteen minutes during the day when you can focus on negative thoughts and complaints. Although this may seem counterproductive, scheduling time to focus on negative thoughts is a technique that can provide a greater sense of control over your thought patterns and allow you to focus on more constructive ideas during the rest of the day (Sharoff 2002). Another powerful way of leaving your inner complainer behind is to focus on the blessings in your life—to approach life with gratitude.

WHAT IS GRATITUDE?

Gratitude has been extolled for thousands of years by major world religions, philosophers, and people with a talent for coming up with pithy quotes. In the first century BCE, the Roman statesman Cicero famously proclaimed, "Gratitude is not only the greatest of virtues but the parent of all the others." Many believe gratitude is worth striving for, but what is it?

Gratitude can be defined as "a sense of thankfulness and joy in response to receiving a gift" (Emmons and Hill 2001, 15). It is often characterized as a complex emotion because it does not yield a recognizable facial expression or a uniquely identifiable pattern of activity in the brain (Solomon 2004). Although gratitude has an emotional component, it also involves a particular way of thinking. Emmons (2007) noted that gratitude has two components: first, noticing and acknowledging what is good in your life and, second, understanding that the goodness comes from a source beyond yourself.

One of the greatest things about gratitude is that you can practice it at any age and under any circumstances. This became apparent to the first-year college students enrolled in a seminar Mark taught that examined how people flourish during difficult times. One of the class assignments required students to give a presentation in the community on the topic of gratitude. They split into two groups to complete the assignment.

Half of the students presented to people enrolled in a program that Crystal developed on campus. The program allows adults with disabilities (Down's syndrome, autism, cerebral palsy, traumatic brain injuries) to attend college lectures. The students asked the adults with disabilities to describe what they were grateful for. One gentleman, who had limited mobility and impaired speech, shared how deeply grateful he was for the members of his family and how much he valued spending time with them. Others expressed gratitude for their friends and teachers. One individual spoke passionately about how he was grateful for two particular video games.

The other half of Mark's class presented to fourth grade students at a local elementary school. The fourth graders also easily identified what they were grateful for. Many of the fourth graders said they were grateful for a parent, a sibling, or a grandparent. One child reported that she was grateful for her frog, guinea pig, three birds, two hamsters, and turtle. Another child expressed gratitude for his ducks. When questioned further, he claimed that his family had 300 of them! Another child was thankful for hockey rinks.

The ability of the children and the adults with disabilities to readily identify and eloquently express what they were grateful for made a deep impression on us. We were reminded that gratitude is possible at any age and when facing any number of substantial physical, emotional, and social challenges.

WHY PRACTICE GRATITUDE?

Without a doubt, focusing on gratitude when you're going through a difficult divorce can seem like a tall order. But with some practice, you can learn to do it. Keep in mind that paying attention to what you're grateful for doesn't mean you have to deny or ignore the pain you are experiencing. It just means that you are broadening your perspective on your circumstances. Rather than focusing on your hardships, you examine your life through a comprehensive lens that identifies blessings in the midst of hardships. Doing this has many benefits.

Gratitude can enhance other positive emotions. Research has shown that focusing on gratitude can increase positive feelings (Emmons and McCullough 2003) and enhance a sense of well-being (Rash, Matsuba, and Prkachin 2011).

Gratitude relates to better sleep. Sleep difficulties, which are common when facing a life stressor such as a divorce, can make you feel miserable. Evidence suggests that an attitude of gratitude relates to better sleep (Wood et al. 2009) and that the practice of gratitude journaling can improve sleep quality (Digdon and Koble 2011).

Gratitude relates to less burnout. Have you experienced job burnout recently? The emotional toll of going through a divorce can spill over to the workplace. Research has shown that gratitude for your job relates to greater job satisfaction and less burnout (Lanham et al. 2012).

Gratitude may strengthen relationships. Research has shown that when people are grateful, they're more likely to include their benefactors in future activities, even if there is a cost to themselves (Bartlett et al. 2012). This may help to build and strengthen relationships.

ENHANCING YOUR ATTITUDE OF GRATITUDE

Reading about gratitude can be intellectually stimulating and inspiring, but if you want it to improve your life, you have to put gratitude into practice. There are many ways to do this.

Identifying People Who Have Made a Difference

Sometimes it's easy to take people for granted who've been helpful during trying times. The next exercise asks you to reflect on the people who have made a positive difference in your life. Make a special point to identify anyone who supported you during your divorce.

EXERCISE 8.2: Identifying People for Whom You're Grateful

GOAL   The goal of this exercise is to spend time thinking about people in your life for whom you're grateful. List people whom you've relied upon for support during your divorce as well as those who've made a difference at other times.

INSTRUCTIONS   In the left column, list people for whom you're grateful. In the right column, briefly describe the reasons for your gratitude toward each person.

Name of Person	Reason(s) for Being Grateful for This Person

Reflection   Look back over your list. Of the people you listed who are still in your life, how long has it been since you spent time with them or gave them a call? Following a divorce, it is especially important to keep in close touch with people who care about you.

Consider adding to this list as new people come into your life.

Expressing Your Thanks

Identifying people to whom you're grateful is a good start. However, if you never let them know how much they mean to you, both of you are missing out on an enriching experience. William Arthur Ward said, "Feeling gratitude and not expressing it is like wrapping a present and not giving it." The wonderful thing about expressing gratitude is that it doesn't cost you anything, and it may have deep and lasting payoffs for both you and the person you're thanking. It's also one of the best ways to quiet your inner complainer.

In his book *Authentic Happiness*, Martin Seligman (2002) recommends writing a gratitude letter to someone who means a lot to you but whom you've never adequately thanked. Seligman asked his students to engage in this task and was struck by the powerful impact that it had on both the writers and the letter recipients.

Mark's seminar students reported a similar experience after being assigned to write a gratitude letter, share it with the other person, and reflect on the experience. Several students reported that they felt a little anxious when they started the assignment because they weren't used to expressing deep feelings of gratitude in such a direct way. However, after they began to share the letters, their anxiety shifted to a feeling of joy when they realized how deeply their letters affected the recipients.

One student noted that she had always admired an older brother who had served as a father figure to their younger siblings after their father had died. Sharing her gratitude letter with her brother affected them both deeply. Upon receiving the letter, her brother said that it was just the boost he needed at the end of what had been a particularly difficult week. Another student wrote a letter to a roommate who had helped her during the transition to college. As soon as the roommate began to read the letter, she began to cry. By the time she was done, the two women were both reaching for the box of tissues. This is a powerful exercise, and we invite you to give it a try.

EXERCISE 8.3: Writing a Gratitude Letter

GOAL   The goal of this exercise is to express your thanks in a letter to someone who has made a positive difference in your life.

INSTRUCTIONS FOR PART A   Select someone you identified in exercise 8.2 who has made a positive difference in your life. Write a letter to this person expressing your gratitude. Your letter can be typed or handwritten and can be as long or as short as you would like.

KEEP IN MIND   Sometimes people feel a little awkward writing this letter because they are trying so hard to say what they feel the right way. Try not to worry about writing the perfect letter. The most important thing is that the words come straight from your heart.

Dear _____,

_____

_____

_____

_____

_____

_____

_____

_____

_____

_____

_____

_____

INSTRUCTIONS FOR PART B   Now that you've written the letter, the next step is to share what you've written with the person. Seligman recommends that you share the letter face-to-face when possible. However, if this is not possible, you could have a conversation over the phone or through video conferencing.

KEEP IN MIND   Sharing your gratitude letter can be an intensely emotional experience (in a good way). It also can be a little anxiety provoking if you aren't used to expressing your gratitude like this. If you're willing to share the letter, you'll likely discover that both you and the recipient are deeply touched.

REFLECTION   In the space provided, describe what it was like for you to write and share your gratitude letter. Do you think you will write other gratitude letters in the future?

_____

_____

_____

_____

_____

_____

_____

_____

Did this exercise have a positive impact on you? If so, it would be consistent with what researchers have discovered. Toepfer, Cichy, and Peters (2012) found that people who wrote three gratitude letters over a three-week period showed greater happiness and life satisfaction and less depression than people who did not write gratitude letters over the same period.

Finding Gratitude in the Simple Things

Since your divorce, how often have you savored an excellent meal, enjoyed a hearty laugh with friends, or noticed the beauty in nature? Learning to take time to appreciate the simple things is an important skill that can serve you well as you try to cope with your divorce. One of the benefits of maintaining a mindfulness practice (see chapter 2) is that you'll feel greater appreciation for the simple joys of life.

Take a moment to think of three things in your life that give you great pleasure. Mark thinks of music, hiking trails, and Ben & Jerry's ice cream. Crystal thinks of her DVR, coffee, and her pug named Bugg. (Yes, that's really her dog's name.) Just thinking about things that give you pleasure can make you feel good.

Practicing Gratitude During Trying Circumstances

It's easier to acknowledge and express gratitude when feeling good. What about expressing gratitude during the difficult times? When life's storm clouds are especially dark and ominous, can you identify a silver lining? Can you see the glass as being half full instead of half empty? Can you make lemonade out of lemons? (Can we cram any more clichés into this paragraph?)

The students in Mark's seminar encountered a fourth grader who was especially good at identifying her blessings. When asked if she had anything to complain about, she answered, "Having to share a room with my younger sister." When asked later what she was grateful for, she replied without hesitation, "Bunk beds." That's a way to find something positive in a difficult situation!

Some people can easily identify the blessings in difficult situations, whereas for others the task is more difficult. If doing this comes naturally to you, it might be an example of what positive psychology researchers call a *signature strength*. But even if identifying blessings is hard for you, you can improve with practice. In the next exercise, we invite you to make a list of complaints or difficult situations that you're currently facing and then see if you can identify any silver linings.

EXERCISE 8.4: Searching for Blessings In Stormy Weather

GOAL   The goal of this exercise is to think about blessings that are present in challenging or difficult situations.

INSTRUCTIONS In the left column, make a list of difficult situations that you're currently facing. Try to be specific. For instance, if you're having trouble adjusting to your divorce, break this down into a specific list of problems (such as *I'm having difficulties paying the bills*, *I miss my old house*, or *I'm feeling lonely*). In the right column, list any blessings that are present in each situation.

KEEP IN MIND Focusing on blessings in challenging situations doesn't mean that you ignore or deny the pain you are experiencing. It just means you are broadening your perspective to incorporate blessings. If you're encountering a lot of inner resistance to this task, you might want to skip it for now. Do this exercise only when you are ready.

Challenging Situation	Blessing(s) That Are Present
Example: *I'm lonely without a romantic partner.*	*I have more time to reconnect with my friends and pursue activities that are important to me.*

REFLECTION   Was finding the silver linings easy or hard to do? On a scale of 1 (extremely easy) to 10 (extremely difficult), how challenging was this task for you?

_____

If you found this exercise to be difficult, keep in mind that you'll get better the more you do it! Before you know it, your inner gratitude voice will be drowning out your inner complainer when times are tough.

Making Gratitude a Daily Habit

Psychologists Robert Emmons and Michael McCullough (2003) tried to answer a simple question: can counting your blessings on a regular basis have a positive impact on your life? They conducted three studies: two with college students and one with adults suffering from a neuromuscular disease. Participants who were assigned to keep a gratitude journal showed greater optimism, sense of well-being, and positive mood than those who kept a different type of journal or who did no writing.

The next exercise invites you to keep a gratitude journal.

EXERCISE 8.5: The Daily Gratitude Journal

GOAL   The goal of this exercise is to work on practicing gratitude on a daily basis.

INSTRUCTIONS   Over the next three days, spend ten to fifteen minutes at the end of each day reflecting upon what you are grateful for. Any blessing during the day would be suitable. You can either list up to five things you're grateful for (as the participants in Emmons and McCullough's study did) or write a paragraph about your gratitude.

Day of the Week	Reason(s) for Being Grateful
DAY 1	
DAY 2	
DAY 3	

REFLECTION　How did you feel when you were thinking about what you are grateful for? Did your mood change? Do you think keeping a gratitude journal is something you'd like to incorporate into your everyday life?

As we mentioned earlier in the chapter, enhancing your attitude of gratitude may strengthen other positive feelings. Our own research suggests that there may be benefits to keeping a gratitude journal following a divorce (Rye et al. 2012). We found that participants who kept a gratitude journal for ten days after attending a workshop on forgiveness improved more on forgiveness of their exes than those who kept a daily events journal following the workshop or those who were assigned to a waiting list.

Identifying a Gratitude Partner

Is there someone in your life who you usually complain to? In other words, do you have a complaint partner? Not that there's anything wrong with that. However, you might consider identifying someone who could be your gratitude partner. A gratitude partner is someone who shares your goal of acknowledging and talking about the blessings in life. It's like having an exercise partner to motivate you to meet your goals. As with any exercise, it can be harder to stick to your gratitude goals if you don't have someone to encourage you on the days you're struggling. The practice of gratitude can be hard, especially when you're experiencing difficulties related to your divorce.

There are many creative ways to find a gratitude partner. One of our colleagues—a divorced parent—used to ask her children every night at the dinner table to say one thing that they were thankful for. Although her children are grown now, they still cherish this tradition and have continued this practice with their own families. Alternatively, you could seek out a close friend or a sibling as a gratitude partner. Make sure to pick someone close who will encourage and inspire you during difficult times.

Using Technology to Enhance Gratitude

You can use technology to help you develop a more grateful perspective. For instance, you might consider setting the alarm on your smartphone to go off at regular intervals throughout the day as a reminder to take a moment to consider what you are thankful for. Or you can download an app that prompts you to keep a gratitude journal. If your gratitude partner lives some distance away, you could use text messages or video conferencing to encourage each other to keep working on gratitude. You could also make a point of expressing gratitude through social media sites. Who knows? It could go viral.

WHAT'S NEXT?

This chapter has addressed how approaching life with gratitude can enhance other positive emotions. Now it's time to focus on something that everyone is seeking after they've been through a divorce—happiness.

CHAPTER 9

"Can I Ever Be Happy Again?"

Yes!

The truth is that none of us are very good at predicting what will make us happy. We spend time and energy chasing after things we think will bring us happiness, only to discover there's still something sorely lacking in our lives. If you still haven't found what you're looking for, you're certainly not alone.

When dealing with divorce, it can be tempting to seek things that provide temporary pleasure but that don't contribute to your happiness over the long term. Seeking temporary pleasure is not necessarily a problem, but at the same time, it's important to develop strategies for rediscovering happiness that will last.

Chapter Focus

This chapter addresses the search for happiness following a divorce. It begins by examining what it means to be happy and why you may not be good at predicting what will make you happy. Drawing upon positive psychology research findings, we provide some suggestions for cultivating happiness. We also offer a few concluding thoughts about using positive psychology strategies to cope with divorce.

WHAT HAPPINESS MEANS

You know happiness when you feel it, you probably spend a lot of time pursuing it—and when you're happy and you know it, you may clap your hands. But what does being happy really mean? Before moving ahead, we invite you to explore this question.

EXERCISE 9.1: What Is Happiness?

GOAL   The goal of this exercise is to explore your personal definition of happiness.

INSTRUCTIONS   Ask yourself what happiness means to you. Reflect on this question in the space provided.

What Happiness Means to You

_____

_____

_____

_____

_____

Now that you've reflected on your own definition of happiness, we'd like to share a few definitions provided by some of the heavy hitters in the field of positive psychology. Sonja Lyubomirsky (2008) defines happiness as "the experience of joy, contentment, or positive well-being, combined with a sense that one's life is good, meaningful, and worthwhile" (32).

Martin Seligman (2002) believes that happiness can be sought on three paths: the pleasant life, the good life, and the meaningful life. The pleasant life is one in which positive emotions are sought through pleasing sensory experiences. The good life involves discovering and using your signature strengths to enhance your own and other's lives.

Finally, the meaningful life entails cultivating a deeply fulfilling existence by capitalizing on your strengths and virtues for the greater good.

Both Lyubomirsky and Seligman emphasize that people actively construct positive emotional states and a meaningful existence. Happiness doesn't just happen to you—you create your own happiness over time. Now that's news to be happy about!

So why is it tough to predict what will make you happy?

ADAPTING TO MAJOR LIFE CHANGES

Consider what happens when you step into a tub of hot water. The change in temperature is initially experienced as uncomfortable. However, over time, your sensory system begins to adapt, and you experience the warmth of the water as being relaxing and pleasurable. The water temperature hasn't changed much, but your body has adapted.

Similarly, research has shown that people adapt emotionally to major transitions in their lives. For instance, many people expect to be happier after marriage, but is that really the case? Using data from a fifteen-year longitudinal study of people living in Germany, Lucas et al. (2003) studied individuals who were initially unmarried but who became and remained married during the course of the study. Participants showed an initial increase in happiness after getting married, but by the end of two years, their happiness had returned to premarriage levels. Keep in mind that these findings reflect average changes that occurred, and some participants experienced lasting changes (both positive and negative). However, in general, participants adapted to their life transitions, and satisfaction levels returned to baseline over time. People also tend to adapt to difficult events, such as divorce.

The tendency for the intensity of feelings to diminish following major life events is called *hedonic adaptation* (Frederick and Loewenstein 1999). Knowing about hedonic adaptation can help you avoid unrealistic expectations. For example, if you expect that a new romantic relationship or marriage will necessarily make you a happier person, you may be setting yourself up for disappointment. Then again, if you doubt whether you will ever feel better again after your divorce, you can take comfort in the fact that over time your mood is likely to improve. In fact, you don't have to passively wait for this to happen. You can take action to improve your mood.

One factor that can significantly impact your mood following a divorce is financial distress. In a consumerist culture, money and happiness are often conflated, and divorce can affect both your wallet and your heart. The next section provides some happiness-promoting strategies that address your financial outlook.

181

HAPPINESS AND MONEY

Financial challenges following a divorce can be daunting. If you're deeply worried about how you're going to pay the lawyer, court costs, alimony, child support, mortgage or rent, car expenses, and medical bills, you aren't alone. Many feel a sense of loss over how their financial outlook has changed. Financial burdens are especially tough to cope with if your ex is trying to squeeze every last penny from you. Perhaps you can relate to the person who exclaimed, "I am having an out-of-money experience!" Financial challenges following a divorce don't have to consume your life or define your path forward, however. There are answers.

Get good financial advice. If you're feeling overwhelmed by your financial burdens, try not to be hard on yourself. Instead, focus your energy on seeking sound advice. There's help available if you're drowning in bills and debt. Consider consulting with a financial planner, reading books on managing finances after divorce, and joining a divorce support group where you can talk about your financial struggles with others.

Spend money on others. There's evidence that spending money on others can boost your happiness. Dunn, Aknin, and Norton (2008) asked participants to rate their happiness in the morning and then gave them an envelope containing money. One group of participants was instructed to spend the money on themselves before 5:00 p.m., and the second group was instructed to spend the money on a gift for another person or to give it to a charitable organization. When the researchers contacted participants that evening, they found that those who had spent money on others reported a significantly higher level of happiness than those who had spent money on themselves.

Spend money on experiences instead of things. If your purchasing power has dropped since your divorce, try to focus on enriching experiences that your money can still buy rather than on material things you cannot afford. "Perhaps the most direct and most reliable way to maximize the happiness and fulfillment that we can extract from money is through need satisfying pursuits—for example, by spending our capital on developing ourselves as people, on growing, and on investing in interpersonal connections" (Lyubomirsky 2013, 173).

The Case of Demarcus

After his divorce from Lynda, Demarcus had been feeling squeezed financially. Demarcus believed that the distribution of finances by the court after his divorce was deeply unfair. Lynda made more money, and Demarcus couldn't buy things for his daughter in the same way Lynda could. Although this situation was difficult, Demarcus was determined to make the most out of his limited resources. Instead of using money to buy his daughter material possessions, he decided to invest in fun, low-cost experiences that he and his daughter could enjoy together. Since then, they have gone cross-country skiing in the local park, played video games, watched matinee movies, and attended free outdoor concerts. Their relationship has strengthened, and Demarcus's daughter undoubtedly will have many wonderful memories of the times that she spent with her father.

Developing a new perspective on money can help you increase your happiness after divorce. In the section that follows, we discuss other strategies you might try in your pursuit of happiness.

OTHER STRATEGIES FOR INCREASING HAPPINESS

Each chapter up to this point has provided strategies designed to enhance well-being, peace of mind, and contentment in your new postdivorce life. We've covered strategies for becoming more aware of your emotional landscape (chapter 1), and for cultivating mindfulness (chapter 2) and self-compassion (chapter 3). To help you deal with hurtful events of the past, we discussed how to move toward forgiveness of others (chapters 4 and 5) and yourself (chapter 6). You've learned about and engaged in work that can infuse your day-to-day life with meaning (chapter 7) and gratitude (chapter 8). But, you're not done yet! We've still got a few more happiness-boosting methods up our sleeves.

Going with the Flow

Going with the flow takes on new meaning when you consider the work of psychologist Mihaly Csíkszentmihályi (1990, 1997). He describes *flow* as an intrinsically rewarding state that comes from intense engagement in an activity. It occurs when you do something just for the sake of doing it, becoming completely absorbed in it. Finding flow in your everyday life can be like taking a minivacation. You are seemingly transported out of your day-to-day existence into a zone where your heart, mind, and body are focused on a rewarding and fun activity. When you're in the groove, there's no room for anxiety and worry!

According to Csíkszentmihályi (1990), here are some of the main elements of flow experiences:

- A challenging activity requiring skills that you are likely to be able to complete

- Clear goals and feedback

- Concentration on the task at hand

- A sense of control over the outcome of the activity

- Loss of self-consciousness

- Altered sense of time, in which time seems to speed up or slow down during the activity

While you can experience a subset of these states, the deep enjoyment characterized by flow includes all of them.

Many activities can produce flow, such as cleaning the house, playing chess, surfing, knitting, driving, bowling, painting, playing music, dancing, and working. Most people report having flow experiences at least some of the time (Csíkszentmihályi 1997). Flow experiences are associated with improved quality of life (Csíkszentmihályi 1990, 1997), although the exact mechanisms as to how flow relates to feelings of well-being are not entirely understood. If you're lucky, your job produces flow experiences. An old proverb states, "Choose a job you love and you will never work a day in your life."

The following exercise will help you cultivate flow in your life.

EXERCISE 9.2: Finding Flow

GOAL The goal of this exercise is to help you identify activities that may produce flow.

INSTRUCTIONS Do you ever get involved in an activity so deeply that nothing else seems to matter and you lose track of time? Whatever your response—whether the answer is yes or it is no—answer the following questions.

QUESTIONS   If you answered yes to the question above, list the activities where this happens:

_____

_____

_____

_____

_____

If you answered no, make a list of any activities that have one or more of these flow elements: the activity is challenging and requires certain skills; the activity merges action and awareness with clear goals and feedback; you have to concentrate as you engage in the activity; you have a sense of control over the outcome; you lose self-consciousness while you are doing it; you experience an altered state of time.

_____

_____

_____

_____

Generate a list of at least three new activities that you could try and that may produce flow experiences. When you are trying new activities, please remember that it may take some time to master the skills necessary to make it a flow activity.

_____

_____

_____

REFLECTION   If you have experienced flow, how did it feel to you?

_____

_____

_____

_____

Reflect on the amount of flow you have in your life—is it enough? Do you need more flow-producing activities? If you want to have more flow experiences, write down a specific plan for cultivating these experiences. For example, if tennis is an activity that produces flow, when are you going to make time to play tennis? Make sure to list the day, time, and place.

_____

_____

_____

_____

Of the list of new possible flow experiences, which one will you likely try in upcoming weeks? Write down a plan to make it happen.

_____

_____

_____

_____

_____

It's good for you to go with the flow, and we hope you were able to identify some activities that promote flow in your life. Speaking of what's good for you, it's also good to do good for others.

Doing Good Is Good for You

It probably comes as no surprise that being kind and charitable to others can benefit the recipient of the kindness, but it also can be advantageous for you if you are the do-gooder. In a review of the scientific evidence on the connections between altruism, health, and happiness, Stephen G. Post (2005), a professor of preventative medicine, found that when people compassionately engage in charitable helping activities, they are more likely to experience greater well-being, happiness, health, and longevity.

Altruism, the unselfish concern for the welfare of others, is associated with certain behaviors and ways of thinking that are related to better mental and physical health (Post 2005). For example, being kind to others can result in deeper social connections and an active lifestyle that counters isolation and passivity. When you help other people, you're less likely to be preoccupied with your own problems, your positive emotional states tend to rise, and your negative feelings tend to decrease. It appears that harmful emotions get short-circuited through simple acts of kindness! Finally, kind and charitable behaviors toward others can enhance a sense of meaning and purpose.

You don't have be Mother Teresa to do more good in your day-to-day life. (In fact, if your efforts to help others become burdensome or overwhelming, the benefits of altruism may decrease.) Even small acts of kindness can go a long way in fostering social connections and nurturing existing relationships. Helping a coworker carry some boxes, fixing your kid's favorite sandwich for lunch, or paying a sincere compliment to a stranger are all small ways to help make someone's day brighter.

If you're up for a bigger altruism investment, you may want to consider trying some volunteer work that's especially meaningful to you. As you contribute to the community and meet new people, your feelings of isolation and self-focus may decrease. Helping someone learn to read, coaching a child's sports team, and volunteering at a nursing home are just a few of the ways you could demonstrate compassion and care for your fellow human beings. Now that you're divorced, think of some volunteer activity that you may have wanted to do in the past but weren't able to do because of your previous lifestyle. Give it a shot. Take a risk for the greater good!

EXERCISE 9.3: Exploring Altruism

GOAL   The goal of this exercise is to explore feelings and identify activities related to increasing your altruism.

INSTRUCTIONS   Choose one day this week to do at least three kind and charitable acts in your day-to-day life. Don't tell anyone what you're doing. Think of these as random acts of kindness.

CHARITABLE ACTS   Describe the charitable acts you did over the course of the day.

_____

_____

_____

_____

REFLECTION   If you were able to see how others responded to what you did, describe their reactions.

_____

_____

_____

_____

_____

_____

_____

How did you feel while doing the charitable acts? How about afterward?

_____

_____

_____

_____

_____

Strengthening Interpersonal Relationships

Investing in others can result in positive returns for you and the recipients of your kindness. Kindness and generosity are ways of nurturing your existing interpersonal relationships. It's not uncommon for people to take their closest family members and friendships for granted, but part of cultivating happiness is taking care of those relationships that mean the most to you.

Why is it so easy to take those relationships for granted? Some of us may believe that family and close friends will always be there to endure our temper tantrums or bad moods or thoughtlessness. That may be true, but you are bound to have more harmony and peace in your relationships if you treat those closest to you with the same kindness and courtesy you'd show to a complete stranger. What can you do to strengthen your interpersonal relationships?

Be present. A wonderful gift to give someone you care about is your presence—not just your physical presence but your mental presence, too. When your loved ones are talking to you, pay full attention. This is a great way to practice your external mindfulness skills (see chapter 2).

Show compassion. Try to understand your friend or family member's point of view. What's it like to walk in his or her shoes?

Approach others with an open heart. When you're interacting with someone, be aware of judgments or biases that may pop into your head. Notice them, let them go, and then refocus with an open mind and heart on what the other person is saying or doing.

Show appreciation. Letting others know how much you appreciate their thoughtfulness can strengthen your bond with them.

Take time to be together. Relationships can wither from neglect, but investing time in those you care about keeps your connections alive. Find out what your friend or family member enjoys doing and do it with him or her. This doesn't have to be a huge commitment of time. Playing a game, taking a walk, or baking cookies together are just some of the ways in which you can spend quality time with those you care about. We bet you have ideas about how to strengthen your social relationships. The next exercise will help you develop a plan.

EXERCISE 9.4: Strengthening Social Relationships

GOAL   The goal of this exercise is to develop strategies to strengthen your existing social network.

INSTRUCTIONS   Choose one person in your social network on which to focus this exercise. You can repeat this exercise with as many people as you would like.

EXERCISE

Name of the person you selected: _____

Do you take this person for granted? If yes, in what ways?

_____

_____

_____

_____

Drawing on the suggestions in this chapter or coming up with your own ideas, write down three things you can do in the next week to strengthen your connection with this person.

1. _____

_____

2. _____

_____

3. _____

_____

Over the next week, implement your plan.

REFLECTION   How do you feel about implementing your plan? Is there anything that might get in the way? What can you do to address those obstacles?

_____

_____

_____

_____

_____

One of the ways to strengthen your existing bonds with those you care about is to take time to have fun together—to play! Patricia McConnell (2002), an animal behaviorist, notes that the human animal is "paedomorphic" (88). We humans are a Peter Pan species, retaining juvenile characteristics, including a love for play, well into adult years. Unfortunately, adults often don't take the time to play. But, we've got some suggestions that just might inspire you to spend a few minutes in your natural play-loving state!

The Joy of Regression

Several years ago, Kellogg's ran a humorous ad campaign promoting Frosted Flakes as a cereal for adults. In the ads, adults of varying ages, whose identity was obscured through dark lighting, proclaimed that they loved eating Frosted Flakes. The ad reminded viewers that you are never too old to act like a kid.

Obviously, acting like a kid and eating Frosted Flakes is not going to make your divorce-related problems go away. However, allowing yourself to be goofy and reconnect with the little kid within can provide a few fun-filled moments when you're not focused on what's going wrong. Is there something you loved as a child that you no longer do because you're afraid of what the neighbors might think? Are you open to rediscovering the joy that can be found in simple things? Whatever you can do following a divorce to create a little opening for joy to enter into your life is a positive step. Consider these suggestions:

Dance with abandon. Sometime when nobody else is watching, crank up the music and just start dancing. Keep dancing until you can't dance anymore. Call it the crazy divorce dance, if you want. (If you live in an upstairs apartment, however, you might want to skip this one.)

Color with crayons. How long has it been since you've used crayons? Other than your second-grade art teacher, who cares if you can't stay within the lines?

Watch Saturday morning cartoons. Remember those early Saturday mornings spent watching cartoons when you were growing up? (Crystal preferred Looney Tunes, but Mark is convinced that Scooby Doo will never be topped.) Try to forget about the divorce to-do list for a while, turn off the cell phone, veg out in front of the television, and enjoy this simple pleasure.

Roll down a grass-covered hill. Next time you find a hill covered with grass, drop whatever you are doing and start rolling down it. (The next day, schedule an appointment to see your chiropractor.)

Perhaps you can think of other ideas. Whatever activity you choose, make a commitment to rediscover the child within you and take him or her out to play once in a while.

This chapter has offered some concrete ways to cultivate happiness after divorce. We realize it may sound a lot easier than it seems to you now. We'd like to close this chapter with an inspiring story.

The Case of Rebecca

About two years ago, seemingly out of the blue, Rebecca's husband of twenty-five years asked for a legal separation. She was the first to admit that her marriage wasn't ideal, but she and Kyle had successfully raised two sons and built a life together focused on their well-being. Rebecca was devastated. To say that her world had been rocked was an understatement, and she sought therapy early on in the separation.

There were times after Kyle moved out when Rebecca had a hard time getting out of bed. The heartache she felt made it hard to believe that she would ever be happy again. "It is what it is," she'd tell her therapist. But now when Rebecca reflects on her journey after the breakup, she says, "It's a work in progress in terms of happiness, and you've got to choose to be happy."

In spite of the pain she was in, she made a commitment to keep moving forward. Rebecca had so many reasons to choose to be happy—her sons, parents, sister, friends, and a profession that she loves. She worked hard to make peace with and let go of painful past events, change the way she thought about herself and her circumstances, and interact with those she cared about in healthier ways.

Gradually, Rebecca realized that over the years, she had lost the sense of who she was and what actually made her happy. Ironically, the devastating end of her marriage provided her an incredible new beginning, the opportunity to create the life she wanted. Just when she thought life was over, a brand new world emerged in front of her eyes. Looking back, this experience reminds her of the metamorphosis of a caterpillar into a butterfly!

One of the biggest challenges in Rebecca's recovery was learning how to engage in self-care and rediscovering what made her happy. She experimented and started with small things: getting her nails done, reading a novel instead of the grocery ads, having popcorn for dinner if that struck her fancy. Meanwhile, she continued to rely on her faith and be involved with her church, while deepening her commitment to volunteer work. The nature of some of her closest relationships changed—she tried setting healthy boundaries that promoted more balance in her life. Those first steps weren't easy, but she pushed herself to take risks.

Now, Rebecca talks about the inner peace she often feels. Things aren't perfect and life continues to throw curveballs, but the hard work she's done is serving her well. "It is what it is," she says, and then adds with a smile, "and it will become what you make it."

We hope that you find Rebecca's story as inspiring as we do. We understand that when things are rough, it can be a stretch to believe that happiness is within your reach. But it is.

FINAL THOUGHTS

You made it to the end of this book, and we'd like to congratulate you for all of the hard work that you've put into your journey toward healing after divorce!

The most important thing to remember is this: you have the strength and ability to overcome suffering and to thrive after your divorce. Some of the positive psychology strategies discussed in this book may come easier to you than others will. Continue working on the ones you're good at. You can tackle the more difficult ones down the road as you begin to feel better and gain confidence in your skills. You might also find it helpful to revisit the exercises in this book from time to time as you continue down the path toward healing.

It's okay to experience periodic doubts about your ability to cope. It's okay to feel sorry for yourself or to grieve over your losses. It's okay to get angry. It's okay to be anxious. After everything you've been through, it would be surprising if you didn't occasionally have these feelings. If you've been practicing your mindfulness skills (see chapter 2), you'll be able to touch these feelings with your awareness before letting them go. These painful feelings don't have to define you, and they don't have to become extra baggage that you drag around with you.

When you're feeling most vulnerable, reach out. You don't have to suffer alone. The importance of support from friends, family, support groups, or a therapist should not be underestimated. You may also find it helpful to draw upon spiritual or religious coping strategies.

We wish you the very best as you apply positive psychology strategies to help bring about healing after your divorce. Along the way, don't forget to take a moment or two to appreciate the journey you've already traveled and the exciting path that is unfolding before you.

References

Abramowitz, J. S., D. F. Tolin, and G. P. Street. 2001. "Paradoxical Effects of Thought Suppression: A Meta-Analysis of Controlled Studies." *Clinical Psychology Review* 21 (5): 683–703.

Adams, T. 2011. "Karen Green: 'David Foster Wallace's Suicide Turned Him into a "Celebrity Writer Dude," Which Would Have Made Him Wince,'" *The Observer*, April 9. http://www.theguardian.com.

Allen, A., and M. Leary. 2010. "Self-Compassion, Stress, and Coping." *Social and Personality Psychology Compass* 4 (2): 107–18.

Aristotle. 2009. *Nicomachean Ethics*. Translated by C. C. W. Taylor. Oxford: Clarendon Press.

Bartlett, M. Y., P. Condon, J. Cruz, J. Baumann, and D. Desteno. 2012. "Gratitude: Prompting Behaviours That Build Relationships." *Cognition and Emotion* 26 (1): 2–13.

Baumeister, R 1991. *Meanings of Life*. New York: The Guilford Press.

Baumeister, R., E. Bratslavsy, C. Finkenauer, and K. Vohs. 2001. "Bad Is Stronger Than Good." *Review of General Psychology* 5 (4): 323–70.

Beck, A. T. 1979. *Cognitive Therapy and the Emotional Disorders*. New York: Penguin Books.

Bevvino, D., and B. Sharkin. 2003. "Divorce Adjustment As a Function of Finding Meaning and Gender Differences." *Journal of Divorce and Remarriage* 39 (3–4): 81–97.

Bonach, K. 2005. "Factors Contributing to Quality Coparenting: Implications for Family Policy." *Journal of Divorce and Remarriage* 43 (3–4): 79–103.

Burns, D. D. 2000. *The Feeling Good Handbook: Using the New Mood Therapy in Everyday Life.* New York: Quill.

Campbell, K., and D. W. Wright. 2010. "Marriage Today: Exploring the Incongruence Between Americans' Beliefs and Practices." *Journal of Comparative Family Studies* 41 (3): 329–45.

Campbell, T. S., L. E. Labelle, S. L. Bacon, P. Faris, and L. E. Carlson. 2012. "Impact of Mindfulness-Based Stress Reduction (MBSR) on Attention, Rumination and Resting Blood Pressure in Women with Cancer: A Waitlist-Controlled Study." *Journal of Behavioral Medicine* 35 (3): 262–71.

Carson, J. W., K. M. Carson, K. M. Gil, and D. H. Baucom. 2004. "Mindfulness Based Relationship Enhancement." *Behavior Therapy* 35 (3): 471–94.

Crocker, J., and A. Canevello. 2008. "Creating and Undermining Social Support in Communal Relationships: The Role of Compassionate and Self-Image Goals." *Journal of Personality and Social Psychology* 95 (3): 555–75.

Crocker, J., and L. Park. 2004. "The Costly Pursuit of Self-Esteem." *Psychological Bulletin* 130 (3): 392–414.

Csíkszentmihályi, M. 1990. *Flow: The Psychology of Optimal Experience.* New York: Harper and Row.

———. 1997. *Finding Flow: The Psychology of Engagement with Everyday Life.* New York: Basic Books.

Digdon, N., and A. Koble. 2011. "Effects of Constructive Worry, Imagery, Distraction, and Gratitude Interventions on Sleep Quality: A Pilot Trial." *Applied Psychology: Health and Well-Being* 3 (2): 193–206.

Dunn, E. W., L. B. Aknin, and M. I. Norton. 2008. "Spending Money on Others Promotes Happiness." *Science* 319 (5870): 1687–88.

Dweck, C. 2006. *Mindset: The New Psychology of Success.* New York: Ballantine Books.

Emmons, R. A. 2007. *Thanks!: How the New Science of Gratitude Can Make You Happier.* Boston: Houghton Mifflin Company.

Emmons, R. A., and J. Hill. 2001. *Words of Gratitude For Mind Body and Soul.* Philadelphia: Templeton Foundation Press.

Emmons, R. A., and M. E. McCullough. 2003. "Counting Blessings Versus Burdens: An Experimental Investigation on Gratitude and Subjective Well-Being in Daily Life." *Journal of Personality and Social Psychology* 84 (2): 377–89.

Enright, R. 1996. "Counseling Within the Forgiveness Triad: On Forgiving, Receiving Forgiveness, and Self-Forgiveness." *Counseling and Values* 40 (2): 107–27.

Enright, R. D., and R. P. Fitzgibbons. 2000. *Helping Clients Forgive: An Empirical Guide for Resolving Anger and Restoring Hope.* Washington, DC: American Psychological Association.

Exline, J., W. Campbell, R. Baumeister, T. Joiner, J. Krueger, and L. Kachorek. 2004. "Humility and Modesty." In *Character Strengths and Virtues: A Handbook and Classification*, edited by C. Peterson and M. Seligman. New York: Oxford University Press.

Fisher, M., and J. Exline. 2006. "Self-Forgiveness Versus Excusing: The Roles of Remorse, Effort, and Acceptance of Responsibility." *Self and Identity* 5 (2): 127–46.

———. 2010. "Moving Toward Self-Forgiveness: Removing Barriers Related to Shame, Guilt, and Regret." *Social and Personality Psychology Compass* 4 (8): 548–58.

Frankl, V. 1946. *Man's Search for Meaning.* Boston: Beacon Press.

Frederick, S., and G. Loewenstein. 1999. "Hedonic Adaptation." In *Well-Being: The Foundations of Hedonic Psychology*, edited by D. Kahneman, E. Diener, and N. Schwarz. New York: Russell Sage Foundation.

Germer, C. 2009. *The Mindful Path to Self-Compassion: Freeing Yourself from Destructive Thoughts and Emotions.* New York: The Guilford Press.

Gilbert, D. 2006. *Stumbling on Happiness.* New York: Alfred A. Knopf.

Gilbert, P. 2009. *The Compassionate Mind.* Oakland, CA: New Harbinger.

Gordon, K. C., S. Burton, and L. Porter. 2004. "Predicting the Intentions of Women in Domestic Violence Shelters to Return to Partners: Does Forgiveness Play a Role?" *Journal of Family Psychology* 18 (2): 331–38.

Gortner, E., S. S. Rude, and J. W. Pennebaker. 2006. "Benefits of Expressive Writing in Lowering Rumination and Depressive Symptoms." *Behavior Therapy* 37 (3): 292–303.

Grossman, P., L. Niemann, S. Schmidt, and H. Walach. 2004. "Mindfulness-Based Stress Reduction and Health Benefits: A Meta-Analysis." *Journal of Psychosomatic Research* 57 (1): 35–43.

Hall, J., and F. Fincham. 2005. "Self-Forgiveness: The Stepchild of Forgiveness Research." *Journal of Social and Clinical Psychology* 24 (5): 621–37.

Hardwick, C. 2002. *Dear Judge: Children's Letters to the Judge.* 3rd ed. Livingston, TX: Pale Horse Publishing.

Holmgren, M. 1998. "Self-Forgiveness and Responsible Moral Agency." *The Journal of Value Inquiry* 32 (1): 75–91.

———. 2002. "Forgiveness and Self-Forgiveness in Psychotherapy." In *Before Forgiving: Cautionary Views of Forgiveness in Psychotherapy*, edited by S. Lamb and J. G. Murphy. New York: Oxford University Press.

Hutchison, E. 2005. "The Life Course Perspective: A Promising Approach for Bridging the Micro and Macro Worlds for Social Workers." *Families in Society* 86 (1): 143–52.

Ito, T., J. Larsen, N. K. Smith, and J. Cacioppo. 1998. "Negative Information Weighs More Heavily on the Brain: The Negativity Bias in Evaluative Categorizations." *Journal of Personality and Social Psychology* 75 (4): 887–900.

Jacinto, G., and B. Edwards. 2011. "Therapeutic Stages of Forgiveness and Self-Forgiveness." *Journal of Human Behavior in the Social Environment* 21 (4): 423–37.

Jaeger, M. 1998. "The Power and Reality of Forgiveness: Forgiving the Murderer of One's Child." In *Exploring Forgiveness*, edited by R. D. Enright and J. North. Madison, WI: University of Wisconsin Press.

Jain, S., S. L. Shapiro, S. Swanick, S. C. Roesch, P. J. Mills, I. Bell, and G. E. Schwartz. 2007. "A Randomized Controlled Trial of Mindfulness Meditation Versus Relaxation Training: Effects on Distress, Positive States of Mind, Rumination, and Distraction." *Annals of Behavioral Medicine* 33 (1): 11–21.

Kabat-Zinn, Jon. 2004. *Wherever You Go, There You Are.* New York: Hyperion.

———. 2013. *Full Catastrophe Living: Using the Wisdom of Your Body and Mind to Face Stress, Pain, and Illness.* New York: Bantam Books.

Kelly, J. B. 2010. "Risk and Resilience in Children Following Separation and Divorce." Presentation at the New York State Council on Divorce Mediation Preconference, Saratoga Springs, NY, April.

Kessler, R. C., W. T. Chiu, O. Demler, and E. E. Walters. 2005. "Prevalence, Severity, and Comorbidity of Twelve-Month DSM-IV Disorders in the National Comorbidity Survey Replication (NCS-R)." *Archives of General Psychiatry* 62 (6): 617–27.

Kroenke, K., and R. L. Spitzer. 2002. "The PHQ-9: A New Depression Diagnostic and Severity Measure." *Psychiatric Annals* 32 (9): 509–15.

Lambert, N. M., F. D. Fincham, T. F. Stillman, S. M. Graham, and S. R. H. Beach. 2010. "Motivating Change in Relationships: Can Prayer Increase Forgiveness?" *Psychological Science* 21 (1): 126–32.

Lanham, M. E., M. S. Rye., L. Rimsky, and S. R. Weill. 2012. "How Gratitude Relates to Burnout and Job Satisfaction in Mental Health Professionals." *Journal of Mental Health Counseling* 34 (4): 341–54.

Lawler, K. A., J. W. Younger, R. L. Piferi, E. Billington, R. Jobe, K. Edmondson, and W. H. Jones. 2003. "A Change of Heart: Cardiovascular Correlates of Forgiveness in Response to Interpersonal Conflict." *Journal of Behavioral Medicine* 26 (5): 373–93.

Lawler, K. A., J. W. Younger, R. L. Piferi, R. L. Jobe, K. A. Edmondson, and W. H. Jones. 2005. "The Unique Effects of Forgiveness on Health: An Exploration of Pathways." *Journal of Behavioral Medicine* 28 (2): 157–67.

Lewis, C. S. 1952. *Mere Christianity*. San Francisco: HarperCollins Publishers.

Lucas, R. E., A. E. Clark, Y. Georgellis, and E. Diener. 2003. "Reexamining Adaptation and the Set Point Model of Happiness: Reactions to Changes in Marital Status." *Journal of Personality and Social Psychology* 84 (3): 527–39.

Luskin, F. 2002. *Forgive for Good: A Proven Prescription for Health and Happiness*. San Francisco: HarperCollins Publishers.

Lyubomirsky, S. 2008. *The How of Happiness*. New York: Penguin Books.

———. 2013. *The Myths of Happiness*. New York: Penguin Books.

Macaskill, A. 2012. "Differentiating Dispositional Self-Forgiveness from Other-Forgiveness: Associations with Mental Health and Life Satisfaction." *Journal of Social and Clinical Psychology* 31 (1): 28–50.

Maltby, J., A. Macaskill, and L. Day. 2001. "Failure to Forgive Self and Others: A Replication and Extension of the Relationship Between Forgiveness, Personality, Social Desirability and General Health." *Personality and Individual Differences* 30 (5): 881–85.

Mauger, P., J. Perry, T. Freeman, and D. Grove. 1992. "The Measurement of Forgiveness: Preliminary Research." *Journal of Psychology and Christianity* 11 (2): 170–80.

McCabe, C. 2013. "Forgiveness and Coping with Divorce." Unpublished manuscript, Skidmore College.

McConnell, P. 2002. *The Other End of the Leash*. New York: Ballantine Books.

McCullough, M. E., K. I. Pargament, and C. E. Thoresen. 2000. "The Psychology of Forgiveness: History, Conceptual Issues, and Overview." In *Forgiveness: Theory, Research, and Practice*, edited by M. E. McCullough, K. I. Pargament, and C. E. Thoresen. New York: The Guilford Press.

McCullough, M. E., E. L. Worthington Jr., and K. C. Rachal. 1997. "Interpersonal Forgiving in Close Relationships." *Journal of Personality and Social Psychology* 73 (2): 321–36.

Neff, K. D. 2003. "The Development and Validation of a Scale to Measure Self-Compassion." *Self and Identity* 2 (3): 223–50.

———. 2011. *Self-Compassion: Stop Beating Yourself Up and Leave Insecurity Behind.* New York: HarperCollins Publishers.

Neff, K. D., and S. N. Beretvas. 2013. "The Role of Self-Compassion in Romantic Relationships." *Self and Identity* 12 (1): 78–98.

Neff, K. D., and C. K. Germer. 2013. "A Pilot Study and Randomized Controlled Trial of the Mindful Self-Compassion Program." *Journal of Clinical Psychology* 69 (1): 28–44.

Nhat Hahn, Thich. 1991. *Peace Is Every Step: The Path of Mindfulness in Everyday Life.* New York: Bantam Books.

Park, C. 2010. "Making Sense of the Meaning Literature: An Integrative Review of Meaning Making and Its Effects on Adjustment to Stressful Life Events." *Psychological Bulletin* 136 (2): 257–301.

Park, C., and S. Folkman. 1997. "Meaning in the Context of Stress and Coping." *Review of General Psychology* 1 (2): 115–44.

Post, S. 2005. "Altruism, Happiness, and Health: It's Good to Be Good." *International Journal of Behavioral Medicine* 12 (2): 66–77.

Prochaska, J. O., and C. C. DiClemente. 1984. *The Transtheoretical Approach: Crossing Traditional Boundaries of Therapy.* Homewood, IL: Dow Jones Irwin.

Pyszczynski, T., J. Greenberg, S. Solomon, J. Arndt, and J. Schimel. 2004. "Why Do People Need Self-Esteem? A Theoretical and Empirical Review." *Psychological Bulletin* 130 (3): 435–68.

Raes, F., E. Pommier, K. D. Neff, and D. Van Gucht. 2011. "Construction and Factorial Validation of a Short Form of the Self-Compassion Scale." *Clinical Psychology and Psychotherapy* 18 (3): 250–55.

Rash, J. A., M. K. Matsuba, and K. M. Prkachin. 2011. "Gratitude and Well-Being: Who Benefits the Most from a Gratitude Intervention?" *Applied Psychology: Health and Well-Being* 3 (3): 350–69.

Riek, B. M., and E. W. Mania. 2012. "The Antecedents and Consequences of Interpersonal Forgiveness: A Meta-Analytic Review." *Personal Relationships* 19 (2): 304–25.

Ross, S., A. Kendall, K. Matters, T. Wrobel, and M. S. Rye. 2004. "A Personological Examination of Self- and Other-Forgiveness in the Five-Factor Model." *Journal of Personality Assessment* 82 (2): 207–14.

Rye, M. S., A. M. Fleri, C. D. Moore, E. L. Worthington Jr., N. G. Wade, S. J. Sandage, and K. M. Cook. 2012. "Evaluation of an Intervention Designed to Help Divorced Parents Forgive Their Ex-Spouse." *Journal of Divorce and Remarriage* 53 (3): 231–45.

Rye, M. S., C. D. Folck, T. A. Heim, B. T. Olszewski, and E. Traina. 2004. "Forgiveness of an Ex-Spouse: How Does It Relate to Mental Health Following a Divorce?" *Journal of Divorce and Remarriage* 41 (3–4): 31–51.

Rye, M. S., K. I. Pargament, W. Pan, D. W. Yingling, K. A. Shogren, and M. Ito. 2005. "Can Group Interventions Facilitate Forgiveness of an Ex-Spouse?: A Randomized Clinical Trial." *Journal of Consulting and Clinical Psychology* 73 (5): 880–92.

Sbarra, D., H. Smith, and M. Mehl. 2012. "When Leaving Your Ex, Love Yourself: Observational Ratings of Self-Compassion Predict the Course of Emotional Recovery Following Marital Separation." *Psychological Science* 23 (3): 261–69.

Scherer, M., E. L. Worthington, J. Hook, and K. L. Campana. 2011. "Forgiveness and the Bottle: Promoting Self-Forgiveness in Individuals Who Abuse Alcohol." *Journal of Addictive Diseases* 30 (4): 382–95.

Seligman, M. 2002. *Authentic Happiness: Using the New Positive Psychology to Realize Your Potential for Lasting Fulfillment.* New York: The Free Press.

Sharoff, K. 2002. *Cognitive Coping Therapy.* New York: Brunner-Routledge.

Smedes, L. B. 1996. *The Art of Forgiving: When You Need to Forgive and Don't Know How.* Nashville: Moorings.

Smith, T. W., K. Glazer, J. M. Ruiz, and L. C. Gallo. 2004. "Hostility, Anger, Aggressiveness, and Coronary Heart Disease: An Interpersonal Perspective on Personality, Emotion, and Health." *Journal of Personality* 72 (6): 1217–70.

Solomon, R. C. 2004. "Forward." In *The Psychology of Gratitude*, edited by R. A. Emmons and M. E. McCullough. New York: Oxford University Press.

Stewart, J. C., G. J. Fitzgerald, and T. W. Kamarck. 2010. "Hostility Now, Depression Later? Longitudinal Associations Among Emotional Risk Factors for Coronary Artery Disease." *Annals of Behavioral Medicine* 39 (3): 258–66.

Suzuki, S. 2006. *Zen Mind, Beginner's Mind.* Boston: Shambhala.

Tabak, B. A., M. E. McCullough, L. R. Luna, G. Bono, and J. W. Berry. 2012. "Conciliatory Gestures Facilitate Forgiveness and Feelings of Friendship by Making Transgressors Appear More Agreeable." *Journal of Personality* 80 (2): 503–36.

Tangney, J., and R. Dearing. 2002. *Shame and Guilt.* New York: The Guilford Press.

Tedeschi, R., and L. Calhoun. 1996. "The Posttraumatic Growth Inventory: Measuring the Positive Legacy of Trauma." *Journal of Traumatic Stress* 9 (3): 455–71.

Thinking Allowed. 1988. "Philosophy in Psychotherapy with Albert Ellis, PhD." Transcript from the series *Thinking Allowed, Conversations on the Leading Edge of Knowledge and Discovery, with Dr. Jeffrey Mishlove.* Interview recorded April 25. http://www.intuition.org/txt/ellis.htm.

Thompson, L., C. Snyder, L. Hoffman, S. Michael, H. Rasmussen, L. Billings, L. Heinze, J. Neufeld, H. Shorey, J. Roberts, and D. Roberts. 2005. "Dispositional Forgiveness of Self, Others, and Situations." *Journal of Personality* 73 (2): 313–60.

Toepfer, S. M., K. Cichy, and P. Peters. 2012. "Letters of Gratitude: Further Evidence for Author Benefits." *Journal of Happiness Studies* 13 (1): 187–201.

Wallerstein, J. S. 1986. "Women After Divorce: Preliminary Report from a Ten-Year Follow-Up." *American Journal of Orthopsychiatry* 56 (1): 65–77.

Wegner, D., D. Schneider, S. Carter, and T. White. 1987. "Paradoxical Effects of Thought Suppression." *Journal of Personality and Social Psychology* 53 (1): 5–13.

Witvliet, C. V. O., T. E. Ludwig, and K. L. Vander Laan. 2001. "Granting Forgiveness or Harboring Grudges: Implications for Emotion, Physiology, and Health." *Psychological Science* 12 (2): 117–23.

Wood, A. M., S. Joseph, J. Lloyd, and S. Atkins. 2009. "Gratitude Influences Sleep Through the Mechanism of Pre-Sleep Cognitions." *Journal of Psychosomatic Research* 66 (1): 43–48.

Worthington, E. L. Jr. 2003. *Forgiving and Reconciling: Bridges to Wholeness and Hope.* Downers Grove, IL: InterVarsity Press.

———. 2013. *Moving Forward: Six Steps to Forgiving Yourself and Breaking Free from the Past.* Colorado Springs: Waterbrook Press.

Worthington, E. L. Jr., C. V. O. Witvliet, P. Pietrini, and A. J. Miller. 2007. "Forgiveness, Health, and Well-Being: A Review of Evidence for Emotional Versus Decisional Forgiveness, Dispositional Forgivingness, and Reduced Unforgiveness." *Journal of Behavior Medicine* 30 (4): 291–302.

Yarnell, L. M, and K. D. Neff. 2013. "Self-Compassion, Interpersonal Conflict Resolutions, and Well-Being." *Self and Identity* 12 (2): 146–159.

Mark S. Rye, PhD, is associate professor of psychology at Skidmore College in Saratoga Springs, NY. He received his PhD in clinical psychology from Bowling Green State University in Bowling Green, OH, and is a licensed clinical psychologist. His research in the field of positive psychology, which focuses on how forgiveness and gratitude relate to mental health, has been funded by the John Templeton Foundation and the Fetzer Institute.

Crystal Dea Moore, PhD, is professor, chair of the department of social work, and holds the endowed Quadracci Chair of Social Responsibility at Skidmore College in Saratoga Springs, NY. She received her PhD in social welfare from the University at Albany, State University of New York, and is a licensed clinical social worker.

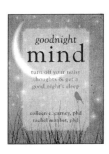
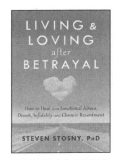

Real change *is* possible

For more than forty-five years, New Harbinger has published proven-effective self-help books and pioneering workbooks to help readers of all ages and backgrounds improve mental health and well-being, and achieve lasting personal growth. In addition, our spirituality books offer profound guidance for deepening awareness and cultivating healing, self-discovery, and fulfillment.

Founded by psychologist Matthew McKay and Patrick Fanning, New Harbinger is proud to be an independent, employee-owned company. Our books reflect our core values of integrity, innovation, commitment, sustainability, compassion, and trust. Written by leaders in the field and recommended by therapists worldwide, New Harbinger books are practical, accessible, and provide real tools for real change.

 **newharbinger**publications